# The Kingdom of God and the Christian Community in Rehoboth

The Sermon on the Mount and its Relevance for the Namibian Church

Thorsten Prill
Heinz Mouton

**Bibliographic information published by the German National Library:**

The German National Library lists this publication in the National Bibliography; detailed bibliographic data are available on the Internet at http://dnb.dnb.de.

ISBN: 9783346324689
This book is also available as an ebook.

Cover image: wikipedia.org

© GRIN Publishing GmbH
Nymphenburger Straße 86
80636 München

Print and binding: Books on Demand GmbH, Norderstedt, Germany
Printed on acid-free paper from responsible sources.

The present work has been carefully prepared. Nevertheless, authors and publishers do not incur liability for the correctness of information, notes, links and advice as well as any printing errors.

GRIN web shop: https://www.grin.com/document/983984

# The Kingdom of God and the Christian Community in Rehoboth

## The Sermon on the Mount and its Relevance for the Namibian Church

Heinz Mouton

Namibian Theological Research Papers

Volume 3

Series Editor: Thorsten Prill

# DEDICATION

I dedicate this book to my late mother, Christa Mouton, and my family.

*After John was put in prison, Jesus went into Galilee, proclaiming the good news of God. "The time has come," he said. "The kingdom of God has come near. Repent and believe the good news!"* (Mark 1:14-15)

# ACKNOWLEDGEMENTS

I am very grateful to all church leaders in Rehoboth who took part in my research.

Heinz Mouton
January 2021

# BIOGRAPHICAL NOTES

**Heinz Mouton** *BTh (Hon), DipTh*
Heinz Mouton is the minister of the *Rynse Kerk Moedergemeente* in Rehoboth. He studied theology at Paulinum United Lutheran Seminary and Namibia Evangelical Theological Seminary in Windhoek.

**Thorsten Prill** *DTh, MTh, PgDipLRM, CThM, Dipl.-Volksw.*
Thorsten Prill is a Crosslinks mission partner and minister of the Rhenish Church in Namibia. He has been seconded by his church to serve as vice-principal at Edinburgh Bible College.

# CONTENTS

# Foreword

Like in most parts of Namibia, Christianity plays a major role in the Rehoboth community. The goal of Christian ethics in any community is to glorify God. Many people in Rehoboth would agree with that statement, in principle. However, as Heinz Mouton's research shows, Pentecostal and mainline Protestant preachers in Rehoboth offer little-to-no ethical application of key passages, such as Jesus' Sermon on the Mount. Mouton argues that this, in part, explains why the lifestyles of many Rehoboth Christians differ significantly from the ethical values of God's Kingdom recorded in the New Testament. His plea to the Rehoboth church, therefore, is for stronger teaching and preaching that emphasises the ethics of Christ's Kingdom, and how they touch all aspects of human relationships: from the workplace, to the neighbourhood, to the family home.

Thorsten Prill
Edinburgh, January 2021

# CHAPTER ONE
## Introduction

### The Christian Community in Rehoboth

The Christian Church has always been and still is an integral part of community life in Rehoboth, which was founded as a mission station by German missionary Heinrich Kleinschmidt in 1845 (Buys & Nambala 2003:19). In her book *Rehoboth, Namibia: Past and Present* Cornelia Limpricht (2012:246) writes: 'Religion and religiosity plays and played a major role within the Rehoboth society as being part and parcel of cultural (Christian) identity.' Most of the almost 29,000 people who live in Rehoboth are members of a church. There is a huge variety of churches that can be found in the town. Among them are mainline Protestant churches, Pentecostal churches and the Roman Catholic Church. On the surface, the Rehoboth community has b een shaped by the Christian faith (cf. Zandberg 2009:5).

However, there are many social challenges, which one would not necessarily expect to find to such an extent in a community that claims to trust in Christ and follow the teachings of the Bible. Like in many other parts of Namibia the community in Rehoboth is confronted with poverty, alcoholism, drug abuse, sexual and gender-based violence, prostitution, etc. (see, for example, the CMA Rehoboth Block B Report). The following excerpt from an article published in *The Namibian*, the largest newspaper in the country, gives good insights into some of the challenges:

> The strong arm of the law ruled the town of Rehoboth over the long weekend as the Police arrested 34 people and successfully kept serious incidents of crime and violence at bay. NamPol station commander Inspector Marschelle Diergaardt told The Namibian that during the weekend, the Police conducted a 'clean-up operation' at the town, which landed a number of people in jail and led to the confiscation of several weapons. Diergaardt confirmed that since September 2010, the Rehoboth Police have conducted regular operations on weekends and long weekends to bring alcohol-related crimes under control. Diergaardt said the impact of the operations has been drastic and positive. 'Before September we had three to four murders a

month, we have reached three murders in total in September,' he said. In total 25 shebeens [bars] were closed on Friday and Saturday for operating later than their licences permit. Police arrested 12 people for drinking in public; 16 were arrested for public drunkenness; two were arrested for being in possession of dangerous firearms; two people were arrested for being in possession of dagga, one person was arrested for robbery, one for theft and another was arrested for damage to property (Smith 2011).

From my observations, I have to say that the lifestyles of many church members in Rehoboth do not seem to reflect the ethical standards which are set by the teachings of the scriptures. This is particularly true for the standards which Jesus formulates in his teaching on the Kingdom of God which can be found in his Sermon on the Mount. It is in this sermon that Jesus gives an in-depth description of those who truly belong to God's Kingdom, or in the words of the Africa Study Bible:

> Every kingdom has expectations and duties for its citizens. The same is true for the people of God's Kingdom. People who will inherit the Kingdom of God should display certain conditions and conduct. Jesus gives the "conditions" of those who are and will be in the Kingdom of God in the Sermon on the Mount in Matthew 5 (2016:1428).

In his book, *The Message of the Sermon on the Mount* John Stott (2000:18), an evangelical Anglican theologian, argues that 'Jesus emphasized that his true followers, the citizens of God's kingdom, were to be entirely different from others.' Stott continues: 'They were not to take their cue from the people around them, but from him, and so prove to be genuine children of their heavenly Father' (:18). As the key phrase, Stott identifies Jesus' appeal to his disciples 'Do not be like them.' (:18). Similarly, R.T. France (1999:106) points out that the Sermon on the Mount does not present an ethic for society, i.e. for all human beings, but is addressed to Jesus' disciples. France calls Jesus' teaching in Matthew 5:1 to 7:29 'a manifesto setting out the nature of life in the kingdom of heaven' (:106) while Stephen Dray (1998:49) speaks of an 'outline of authentic discipleship.'

Stanley Hauerwas (1993:153), who agrees that the Sermon on the Mount is addressed to the church and, therefore, does not make any sense to those outside the body of Christ, writes the following about the purpose of Jesus' sermon:

> I want to suggest that the Sermon on the Mount constitutes and is constituted by a community that has learned that to live in this manner requires learning to trust in others to help me so live. In other words, the object of the Sermon on the Mount is to create dependence: It is to force us to need one another (:153).

J. Daryl Charles (2004:49) states that the evangelist Matthew stresses that disciples of Jesus need to be doers of God's will. He notes that 'the ethical contours of righteousness and the necessity of validating the disciple's lifestyle are accentuated' in Mathew's Gospel, and particularly in the Sermon on the Mount (:49). The gap between expectation and reality has prompted me to think about the biblical teaching on the Kingdom of God and its relevance for the churches in my hometown of Rehoboth.

## Research Purpose and Research Questions

The purpose of my research is to find out what Rehoboth church leaders believe and teach about the Kingdom of God and its ethical standards. This will help to explain the obvious discrepancy between Jesus' teachings' in the Sermon on the Mount and the lifestyles and attitudes which we can find in the Rehoboth community. The main research questions are: (1) What are the ethical implications of the Kingdom of God for the Christian community? (2) What do church leaders in Rehoboth think about the lifestyles of Christians in the Rehoboth community and their churches? (3) What do church leaders in Rehoboth believe and teach about the Kingdom of God in general and the ethical standards of the Kingdom as we can find them in Jesus' Sermon on the Mount (Matthew 5:1 -7:29)?

## Working Hypothesis

There is a discrepancy between Jesus' teachings in the Sermon on the Mount and the lifestyles and attitudes of Christians in Rehoboth. Our hypothesis is that this discrepancy is in some way related to the pastors' understanding of God's Kingdom and how they teach or do not teach biblical ethical standards. In other words, there is a general lack of understanding among pastors of Rehoboth regarding the Kingdom of God, which helps to explain the general lack of understanding within the Rehoboth community.

## Research Design and Methodology

The chosen design for this research is that of a quantitative survey among church leaders in Rehoboth (cf. Bryman 2012:470). I constructed a questionnaire which I distributed among leaders of mainline Protestant and Pentecostal churches. The questionnaire contained quantitative questions that helped me to identify what the church leaders believed about God's Kingdom and its ethical standards. Altogether, I produced and distributed forty questionnaires. Seventeen church leaders agreed to fill in the questionnaire. Before I started with the survey study I undertook a pre-test/pilot study (cf. Bryman 2012:260). For this pilot survey, I interviewed one church leader. This helped me to refine the wording of the questions and adjust the questionnaire to ensure the clarity of the survey and the reliability of my research results.

# CHAPTER TWO
# The Kingdom of God and Ethical Living

As the Christian community in Rehoboth is experiencing different kinds of moral crises, this paper will explore the implications of the kingdom ethics of Matthew which seem to be particularly relevant to the Christian community in Rehoboth and to those in other parts of Namibia which are facing similar situations.

## The Meaning of the Kingdom of God

The phrase *Kingdom of God* can be found four times in Matthew's Gospel, fourteen times in Mark's Gospel, thirty-two times in Luke's Gospel and only twice in John's Gospel (Ladd 2001:657). In addition to the four gospels, it occurs six times in the Book of Acts, eight times in the Pauline letters and once in the Book of Revelation. The term *Kingdom of Heaven* is used thirty-three times in Matthew's Gospel. France (1985:46) acknowledges the fact that Matthew characteristically uses the phrase kingdom of heaven, while this term is absent from all other gospels. He believes that Matthew avoids direct reference to God because of his predominantly Jewish readership. France concludes that the meaning of the phrases *Kingdom of God* and *Kingdom of heaven* is synonymous (:46). They are simply linguistic variations of the same concept (Ladd 2001:657). This view is shared by the majority of scholars today. Scott Newman (2010:299), for example, writes: 'The current consensus among scholars is that Matthew uses "kingdom of heaven" rather than "Kingdom of God" as a kind of reverential circumlocution to avoid using the name of God much the same way that a devout Jewish author would write "G-d" instead of "God".'

Joel Green (2013:468-481), however, questions this explanation why the phrase *kingdom of heaven* is used in Matthew's gospel in preference to the term *Kingdom of God*. He points out that Matthew makes use of the word 'God' (*theos*) some fifty times and also uses the phrase *Kingdom of God*. Jonathan Pennington (2007:16) says that the various explanations which are being offered bypass the inquiry into the significance of the term 'of heaven'. He strongly rejects the idea of reverential circumlocution (:36) Instead he argues that 'there are indeed other reasons why Matthew uses 'heaven' rather than 'God' in phrases such as 'kingdom of heaven' (:16). Pennington shows that the term 'heaven' is very prominent in the Old Testament book of Daniel: 'Daniel particularly stands out in its extra use of heaven, nearly all which are used to describe God as a heavenly God with phrases such as "God of heaven"' (:49). Pennington goes on to argue that Matthew prefers the term *Kingdom of heaven* because 'heaven' language plays a significant role in the book of Daniel, which distinguishes between earthly kingdoms and the heavenly kingdom (:285-293). According to Pennington, Daniel 4:34 portrays the king of heaven against the earthly kings. God as the heavenly father is in the heavenly kingdom ruling over the earthly kings and kingdoms. Pennington notes how the first three appearances of the term *kingdom* proclaimed by Jesus and John in Matthew 3:2 and 4:1 are set in stark contrast to 'the entire worldly kingdoms' portrayed by the devil in Matthew 4:8. Consequently, Matthew prefers the phrase *Kingdom of heaven* to emphasize the heavenly origins and nature of the kingdom. Donald A. Carson (2017) comments on Pennington's view:

> Jonathan Pennington [...] has shown that Matthew contrasts "heaven" and "earth" as two spheres, two kingdoms – one that embraces all that is God-centered and good, the other all that is in rebellion and characterized by corruption. By preferring "kingdom of heaven" to "Kingdom of God," Matthew is sustaining this powerful antithesis and drawing attention to the quality of the kingdom that both the Baptist and Jesus announce.

One of the major problems regarding the doctrine of the Kingdom of God is its definition. France (1985:45-46) argues that the definitions of the Kingdom of God do not do justice to the term, but rather restrict it in its breadth. He emphasises that it is important not to limit our understanding of the theme of the Kingdom of God to a specific area of application:

Attempts to define 'the Kingdom of God' inevitably restrict this breadth, and so fail to do justice to the variety of its usage in the Gospels. So, for instance, when the parables of Matthew 13 tell us what 'the kingdom of heaven is like', they are depicting in a variety of contexts what happens when God has his way, when his will is done and his purpose fulfilled. When Jesus tells his disciples to 'seek his kingdom' (6:33) he is telling them to put God first, not prescribing a specific line of action (:46).

Over the centuries, several authors have done a lot of scholarly work on the Kingdom of God and how it influences Christian ethics in light of the Sermon on the Mount. The Kingdom of God is God's sovereign rule manifesting itself in his saving power and cannot be restricted to a particular domain (Cf. Stanton 2001:59). The English word 'kingdom' can be translated as both the authority and the power of a king. Sean Adams (2013:178) argues that the Kingdom of God is a central concern for the gospel writers. The kingdom originates from God (cf. Greidanus 1999:30). It is portraying God's character. It is not dependent upon human beings. However, it invites men and women to receive and enter it (e.g. Mark 10:14-15).

George Eldon Ladd (1993:60) holds that created beings are unable to establish God's Kingdom: 'In any case, throughout all Judaism, the coming of God's Kingdom was expected to be an act of God – perhaps using the agency of human beings – to defeat the wicked enemies of Israel and to gather Israel together, victorious over its enemies, in its promised land, under the rule of God alone.' God's Kingdom is God's reign, i.e. God's rule (:61). This, Ladd (2001:657) argues, is its primary meaning in the New Testament. It is God's authority and rule which God the Son received from God the Father. The former will exercise this rule until he has subdued all enemies of God. Once he has completed that mission Christ will return the kingdom, i.e. his authority as Messiah, to his heavenly Father.

William Barclay (1999:30) describes God's Kingdom not as a domain but as the dominion of God. He continues: 'We can see then that the Kingdom of God does not mean a territory in which God is king; it means a condition of heart and mind and will where God is Lord of all' (:30). France (1995:413), pointing to Matthew 28:18, argues that the kingdom is established in heaven and on earth. Jesus, the king, now receives all authority in heaven and on earth. In Matthew 4:1-11 Jesus was offered all the kingdoms of the earth and their glory, but his obedience and death on the cross purchased far more than what Satan offered. By saying in Matthew 28:18 'All authority in heaven and on earth has been given to me' Jesus refers to Daniel 7:4. Authority is a concept that needs to be understood in the immediate context in which it has been used. Ladd (1959:20) explains that power, might and glory are all expressions of authority. It is noteworthy that all these terms are also synonymous with the kingdom. Thus, in Daniel 2:37 we read, 'You King, the King of Kings, to whom the God of heaven has given the kingdom: the power, might, and the glory'. Similarly, the apostle Paul writes in Ephesians 1:10 that God will 'bring all things in heaven and earth together under one head, even Christ'. Put differently, all the lines of God's revelation meet in Christ; all religion centres in God's Son (Henry 2010:1119). Jews and Gentiles were united to one another by being united to Jesus. Wiersbe (2007:587) comments: 'Sin is tearing everything apart, but in Christ, God will gather everything together in the culmination of the ages.'

The sovereign rule of God is described by Robert Plummer (2010:153) as the idea that God's rule is cemented in his kingship. He explains that in the Old Testament God's kingship is mediated to Israel through the human kings and prophets. However, in the New Testament it is Jesus, the son of David, who declares that God's reign is taking place (:153). Likewise, Ladd (1964:80) says that the Kingdom of God is the sovereign rule of God and it is manifested in the person and work of Christ, creating a people over whom he reigns and issuing a realm or realms in which his power is realized. Herman Ridderbos (1962:9) holds that *malkuth shamaim* (kingdom of Heaven) speaks of a universal rule, i.e. God's sovereignty over all the earth. Kingdom should be understood as rule rather than realm.

In secular use, the phrase 'kingdom' usually refers to a geographical territory, a political entity or a community of people who are ruled by a king. Thus, the Cambridge Dictionary, for example, provides the following definitions: 'A country ruled by a king or queen' and 'An area that is controlled by a particular person or where a particular quality is important'. In his book *Kingdom: The Expression of God's Rule* Christopher Woodall (2012: x) writes that such 'ideas are not entirely absent in relation to God's kingdom'. However, the main meaning of God's Kingdom is a different one. Woodall notes:

> [I]t would perhaps be more accurate to speak of it as the Father's heavenly rule expressed on earth in human lives. In other words, it is the rule of God in action. Moreover, God's kingdom implies his kingship. No room here for strategies devised by men. He is executing a plan according to his own purposes in Jesus Christ (: x).

As we have seen, the idea of God's Kingdom as the rule of God is very prominent in the writings of Ladd. It is also Ladd who stresses that the Kingdom of God is not identical with the Church of Christ (1993:111). While they are closely related to each other they must not be seen as synonymous. Ladd notes:

> The Kingdom is primarily the dynamic reign or kingly rule of God and, derivatively, the sphere in which the rule is experienced. In biblical idiom, the Kingdom is not identified with its subjects. They are the people of God's rule who enter it, live under it, and are governed by it. The church is the community of the Kingdom, but never the kingdom itself. Jesus' disciples belong to the Kingdom as the Kingdom belongs to them, but they are not the Kingdom. The Kingdom is the rule of God; the church is a society of men (:93).

Having said that, the Kingdom of God works through the Church of Christ (Ladd 2001:660). Thus, the New Testament writers tell us how the disciples of Jesus not only preached the kingdom but also performed signs of the kingdom. In the words of Ladd, 'The powers of the kingdom were operative in and through them' (:660).

The Kingdom of God refers to the fact that God is ruling rather than to an area over which he is sovereign. We can see this when we turn to the Book of Psalms. According to Psalm 103:19, God 'has established his throne in the heavens and his kingdom rules over all'. In Psalm 145:11 we read: 'They shall tell of the glory of your kingdom and speak of your might'. Psalm 145:13 stresses that God's kingdom is an everlasting kingdom and that his dominion endures throughout all generations. The Hebrew word for kingdom, i.e. *malkuth,* refers to his reign, his rule and his sovereignty: 'When *malkuth* is used of God, it almost always refers to his authority or to his rule as heavenly king' (Ladd 2002:47). According to Ladd (2002:63), scholars in the past did not agree on the basic meaning of the word (*basileia*) and many interpreted it as the eschaton, i.e. the final eschatological order. Such an interpretation, however, would restrict it exclusively to the future. This understanding would cause problems concerning the present and future view of the Kingdom. Consequently, we can see that the problem of kingdom truths is not solved by offering a vague definition of the Kingdom. The solution lies in the particulars.

## The Kingdom of God and Salvation

All mainline churches in Rehoboth, like the Rhenish Church, the Congregational Church, the Uniting Reformed Church or the Lutheran Church, subscribe to the Apostles' Creed, a creed that clearly speaks of God's salvation and judgement. Indeed soteriology is a theme that is much preached in the churches in Rehoboth. It is also an important aspect of the Christian life that is often discussed. Both Calvinism and Lutheranism emphasise that salvation is accomplished by the almighty power of the triune God (cf. Steele & Thomas 1963:22). Calvinists believe that God has selected a group of people and has chosen his Son to die for them. The work of the Holy Spirit is to make the death of Christ effective by bringing those who have been elected to repentance and faith. Calvinism understands the whole process (election, redemption, and regeneration) as the gracious work of God (cf. Keathley 2010:101ff). However, what is often overlooked is the soteriological aspect of God's Kingdom.

The Old Testament constantly refers to God as the judge of all. The aspect of judgement is an important aspect of all Christian teachings. The Nicene Creed indicates that the task of judgement is given to Jesus. Thus, it states: 'He shall come again, with glory, to judge the quick and the dead; whose kingdom shall have no end' (quoted in Schaff 2010:433). George Beasley-Murray (1992:19) quotes Psalm 99 where the power of God can be seen in both the acts of judgement and salvation. Beasley-Murray describes the kingdom as 'the time when God puts forth his royal powers and establishes his rule of righteousness' which consists of peace and joy for human beings (:19). Ladd (1993:74) in his book *A Theology of the New Testament* acknowledges that salvation is the complete opposite of being lost; being lost portrays destruction or being destroyed. The destruction will be under God's wrath. In Matthew 7:13 we read that the lost will burn in fire and be excluded from the joy and pleasures of the presence of God in his Kingdom. Thus, creation's outcry is salvation from judgment.

Ladd (1993:72) stresses the fact that the Kingdom of God is not only about the reign of God but that it also includes the gift of life and salvation which is achieved through God's reign. Thus, he writes: 'The object of the divine rule is the redemption of people and their deliverance from the powers of evil [...] It brings to people "righteousness, peace and joy" (2001:658). The Kingdom of God is concerned with the whole human being and the restoration of fellowship between God and his human creatures (Ladd 1993:74). The pure in heart in Mathew 5:8 will see God and enter into the joy of the Lord. Jesus urges his disciples to seek the kingdom and its righteousness as one's most valuable possession (Matt 6:33; 13:44-46; Luke 12:31-32). Likewise, David Bickel (2001:2) describes the Kingdom of God as 'God's active rule over his creation', which includes 'saving his creatures from their sins and the consequences of those sins'. Similarly, Beasley-Murray (1989:84-87) defines the Kingdom of God as God's sovereign power to deliver his creation from the destructive powers that are doing their best to ruin it. France (1985:209) points out that the Kingdom of God is not only God's rule over his obedient subjects, but includes his victory over their spiritual enemies through Jesus, beginning in the present age (Matt 12:28; Luke 1:68-75; 11:20). Ladd (1993:91) notes that the prophets' hope of the Kingdom of God was inaugurated in the person of Jesus in this present age. God asserted his rule in history by defeating the devil and death through the work of Jesus; even though God will not complete his display of authority until Jesus returns as the judge of the world when God will start the new world order.

Within Christian theology salvation is clearly understood as entering the Kingdom of God, i.e. as the transfer of men and women from the kingdom of darkness to the kingdom of his Son. Believers in Christ are no longer part of the kingdom of the world (also called the kingdom of Satan), which is opposed to the

Kingdom of God. They become members of 'a chosen race, a royal priesthood, a holy nation, God's own people', as the apostle Peter puts it (1 Peter 2:9). In other words, God's Kingdom is, as Michael Lawson (2000:47) writes, very much a community concept. He explains:

> The New Testament makes clear that those who are brought into the realm of salvation enter in as fellow members of God's family. The people of God are kingdom people because they derive their identity from Christ the King. He is guiding his people to the consummation of history, when he will return in divine power as King and Judge, and as the bestower of eternal blessing for those who have given their full allegiance to him (:147).

## The Kingdom of God and Eschatology

In the 19th century, theologians like Albrecht Ritschl understood the kingdom of God 'as a static realm of moral values, toward which society was steadily advancing through a process of continuous evolution' (McGrath 1998:546). In other words, they saw the kingdom as a humanistic, moral programme that would lead to a better and ultimately perfect society. This view was challenged by Johannes Weiss and Albert Schweitzer towards the end of the 19th century. Schweitzer and Weiss discovered the apocalyptic character of Jesus' preaching and insisted that the Kingdom of God was an eschatological or futurist concept (:546). They argued that 'Jesus' teaching was profoundly Jewish, drenched in intense eschatological hope' (Bock 2004). Weiss held that Jesus' vision of God's kingdom could not be reduced to a moral cause centered on the present life, but must be understood as a wholly future, supernatural and transcendent reality (Houlden 2003:210). Darrell Bock (2004) writes about Weiss' position:

> For Weiss, the kingdom was purely religious, not ethical; purely future, not present in any way. The Kingdom would be God's final miracle with Jesus functioning in his current ministry as *Messias designates*. For Weiss, Jesus believed that he would one day become the Son of Man. At first, Jesus believed that this would occur during his lifetime, and later in his ministry,

he anticipated it to come shortly after His death. This is a heritage that Jesus believed he possessed, though he had not yet entered into it.

Schweitzer agrees with Weiss' position (Fuellenbach 2006:189). He holds that Jesus was expecting the kingdom to come within his lifetime and that he considered himself to be a messenger of the coming kingdom. However, the sending of the twelve disciples ended in a devastating moment when they returned and the apocalypse of the kingdom was still in remission. Joseph Fuellenbach notes:

> With this realisation in mind, he preached its imminent coming, sending his disciple on their mission as recorded in Matthew 10. He did not expect them before the kingdom would come. The failure of the parousia of the Kingdom to place immediately was the turning point of Jesus' ministry. Convinced the pre-messsianic tribulations were transferred by God to the suffering and death of the messenger of the Kingdom, Jesus realized that he had to take upon himself those tribulations expected for the end-time in order for the Kingdom to come (:189).

As a result, the coming of the kingdom is postponed until his second coming. For Schweitzer the second coming of Christ was imminent (Bock 2004). This explains why Schweitzer's priority was to go to Lambaréné in Gabon to establish a hospital. He thought that Christians were called to transform the world which was essentially hostile to a world where love prevailed.

Not all scholars agree with Schweitzer and Weiss. Charles H. Dodd, for example, strongly rejects the idea of a futurist kingdom (McGrath 1998:546). He argues that the Kingdom of God came with Jesus and is known wherever the Lordship of Jesus is acknowledged. Put differently, the kingdom has already come upon people. It has already been realised in the coming of Jesus Christ, i.e. in his life, death and resurrection (:547). What the Old Testament prophets considered as future has already happened in Jesus. Fuellenbach (2006:190) describes Dodd's view well when he writes:

C.D. Dodd proposed his view of the kingdom, which has become known as "realized eschatology." The Kingdom of God as preached by Jesus is a present reality. It is already here. History has become the vehicle of the eternal. This world has become the scene of a divine drama in which the eternal issues are laid bare. It is the hour of decision.

Others like Rudolf Bultmann have tried 'to demythologize Jesus' image of the apocalyptic Kingdom into […] an existential claim for a crisis decision', while Amos Wilder and Norman Perrin turned 'kingdom language into a mere metaphorical symbol of hope and transformation' (Bock 2004). Both approaches are attempts to redefine the meaning of God's Kingdom. Interestingly, both views of the kingdom tend to be rather individualistic. They tend to be self-centric concepts which are exactly what Jesus fought against.

Bultmann stands, as Robert Cubillos (2017:355) writes, in the 'eschatological interpretative tradition with Weiss and Schweitzer agreeing that Jesus made a serious miscalculation concerning the end of the world.' Like Weiss and Schweitzer, he argues that for Jesus the Kingdom of God was an event in the future to be brought about by God. However, his interpretation differs from Weiss and Schweitzer insofar as he sees the Kingdom of God as a power, which, although it is entirely in the future, wholly determines the present. Bultmann holds that the Kingdom of God determines the present because it compels human beings to make a decision, or as Bock (2004) puts it: 'What Bultmann stressed was the crisis of decision Jesus' challenge raised.' Bultmann believes that the kingdom is not a condition realised on earth but an inward conviction of human beings in the here and now (cf. Segal 2006:345). Consequently, Jesus should be viewed as a miraculous event that is inspiring human beings to come to a decision (Morton 2010:83). In other words, the Kingdom of God is not a territory in which God is King; it rather refers to a condition of the heart, mind and will, implying that God is Lord and King of all.

Finally, there are those scholars who support the idea of an inaugurated eschatology. This is the understanding that the present reality starts with the works of Jesus (Matthew 12:28). The kingdom already exists within the lives of Christians. However, there will be a future consummation when God will reign over the full realm of the cosmos. Alister McGrath (1998:547) explains this position well when he writes: 'The kingdom of God has begun to exercise its influence within human history, although its full realization and fulfilment lie in the future.' This *both-present-and-future* or *already/not yet* view which was first formulated by Oscar Cullman and promoted in evangelical circles by George Ladd 'is probably the most prominent view currently in New Testament circles at large, both conservative and critical' (Bock 2004). Ladd (2001) emphasises that this view of the kingdom was taught by Jesus himself. He states: 'Jesus taught that the kingdom, which will come in glory at the end of the age, has come into history in his own person and mission' (:658).

From my observation, it seems that this view has also become a common feature in the Namibian church community. It can be found in Christian catechisms which are currently in use in both Protestant and Roman Catholic churches and is promoted at the theological seminaries in the country. It seems that the present consensus in many Namibian churches is that the Kingdom of God has both a present and future dimension.

As Roger Crook (2016:79) points out such language may come across as rather abstract. This prompts the question, 'What does such an understanding of the kingdom mean for ethical living?' Crook gives the following answer:

> At the heart of the matter is the fact that citizenship in the kingdom imposes on the disciples of Jesus a radical demand for obedience. Those who accept God's offer for forgiveness and become a part of the community of faith have a responsibility to obey. Right and wrong, good and bad are defined by the purposes of God. Every way of acting must be evaluated not in terms of whether it is expedient or logical but in terms of God's will. The believer's decisions about day-today activities must be based on the sovereign will of God (:79-80).

## The Kingdom of God and its Values

While the covenant between God and Israel is central to Old Testament ethics (cf. Wright 1993:22), the Kingdom of God plays a central role in New Testament ethics. James Nkansah-Obrempong (2013:93) notes that Jesus' moral teachings focus on how people who have joined his kingdom should behave and live in their communities (:93). He explains:

> Those who are in the kingdom must live lives that reflect the values of the kingdom of God. For Jesus this kingdom value is not happiness, which is a central value in humanistic and secular ethics but the pursuit of God's kingdom. Humanity is to first seek Gods' kingdom and righteousness (Matt. 6:33). Righteousness is a moral value that must shape our moral life. Another kingdom value is goodness (:94).

Sherwood Lingenfelter (2008:49) identifies servanthood as a core value in God's Kingdom. Referring to encounters between Jesus and some of his disciples which are recorded in the synoptic gospels (i.e. Matthew 18:1-5; Mark 9:35-37; Luke 9:46-48) Lingenfelter states: 'Jesus makes this very clear to his disciples when they are fighting with one another about who is going to be the greatest in the kingdom of heaven.' While servanthood is indeed an important kingdom value, most scholars agree that these accounts point to another central value that is intrinsically linked to servanthood. Thus, Jesus expects his disciples to become not only servants but the 'very last' (Mark 9:35). In other words, he is calling them to be humble servants. Victor Babajide Cole (2006:1187) observes: 'This is a radical tenet of the kingdom of God. Lowliness is the pathway to greatness in the kingdom.' We can find this emphasis on humility also in Matthew 18:1-5. Commenting on this passage Joe Kapolyo (2006:1146) writes:

> Leaders must become like little children. Some commentators have suggested that this means that leaders must have such childlike character-istics as innocence, wonder, dependence, trust and the ability to forgive. While these qualities are important, the most significant quality of the child in this story is that he had no status, no importance, except as a responsibility for others to care for. To become like a child is therefore to

renounce any notions of self-importance and to embrace insignificance. This is true humility (Phil 2:6-11), the prime characteristic of all who follow Jesus.

Jesus' teaching about life in the kingdom clearly focuses on human behaviour. His teachings include the beatitudes (Matt.5:1-11), the blessings and woes (Lk 6:20-26), the golden rule (Mk 7:12), the parable of the narrow and wide gates (Mk 7:13-14; Lk 13:24), the parable of the unmerciful servant (Mk 18:21-35), and the parable of the Good Samaritan (Lk 10:25-37), among others. All these teachings portray ethical living in God's Kingdom. Having said that, ethical kingdom living is best described in Jesus' Sermon of the Mount.

## The Sermon on the Mount and Kingdom Ethics

The Sermon on the Mount forms one of five teaching blocks in Matthew's Gospel (Mt 5–7; 10, 13, 18; 24–25). Each of them closes with a similar refrain: 'and when Jesus had finished' (Talbert 2010:6). Scott McKnight (2014:1) calls Jesus' sermon 'the moral portrait of Jesus' own people.'

In his book, *The Message of the Sermon on the Mount* Stott (2000:18) argues that 'Jesus emphasized that his true followers, the citizens of God's kingdom, were to be entirely different from others, which portrays metanoia (repentance) a paradigm shift of the mind and the righteousness which is part of the Kingdom.' Stott emphasizes that the Sermon on the Mount stresses a constant need to be different. Frederick Bruner (2004:156) points out that there is a theme of imitation: 'Jesus blesses full people who reach out into the world in imitation of the One who has reached down to them.' It is also important to interpret the Sermon on the Mount in proper order. Thus, Martyn Lloyd-Jones (2012) writes the following: 'The Beatitudes do not come at the end, they come at the beginning, and they set up the stage for what follows. There is logic to our Lord's order that must not be ignored.'

The Sermon on the Mount has been widely discussed in Christian literature and scholarly writings since the first circulation of the Gospels. Some feel that the Sermon on the Mount is the foundation for, and a good representation of a strong Christian ethic. For Justin Martyr Jesus' Sermon on the Mount teaches how a true disciple of Jesus must live: 'For we ought not strive; neither has He desired us to be imitators of wicked men, but He has exhorted us to lead all men, by patience and gentleness, from shame and the love of evil' (quoted in Lawrence (2017:16). Likewise, Richard Niebuhr holds that 'Jesus' teachings in the Sermon on the Mount are not merely ideal but actual and practical ethics to be embodied in the community of believers as they seek to show the presence of God's kingdom here and now' (Siker 1997:204). Others, like Johannes Weiss and Albert Schweitzer, suggest that the Sermon on the Mount is an interim ethic, i.e. a temporary way for Christians to live until the second coming of Christ (Collins 2013). The problem of this position is, as Dan Lawson (2009:30) points out, that Jesus' teachings 'might be seen as rules, regulations, and requirements that a believer must rigidly keep to qualify for heaven rather than presenting the teachings of Christ as a way of living that permeates the life of the believer.'

Others think that it is impossible to read the Sermon on the Mount as a manual for personal ethics. Reinhold Niebuhr, for example, believes that 'the ethic of Jesus expressed in the Sermon on the Mount is an impossible ethical ideal of love' (Siker 1997:204). Likewise, Protestant reformer Martin Luther held that the Sermon on the Mount preaches a way of life that cannot be attained by Christian believers. He saw in Jesus' sermon, as Jack Lundbom (2009:441) puts it, 'an impossible ethic designed to awaken us to our inadequacy and sinfulness, which would then drive us to seek God's mercy and help.' Such a view, however, contributes to the fact that Christians often omit the passage and avoid seeking any practical ethical application from the Sermon on the Mount in everyday life. It reduces Jesus' sermon to a *pedagogical device* which he used to reveal human beings as sinners who are in need of salvation (Lawson 2009:30). Hauerwas' criticism is worth quoting in full:

> A more common interpretation is that the Sermon is a law that presents an impossibly high ideal to drive us to a recognition of our sin. It is meant to drive us to grace. In other words, it is not really meant to tell us what to do but rather to remind us that Christian moral life is about love. This inter- nalizes the Christian life so that what it means to be a Christian is to do whatever we do from the motive of love. "Love and do what you will"—

bad advice if I have ever heard it! It has an even worse effect on christology; why would anyone ever have put Jesus to death if it is all just a matter of being loving? (1993:154)

David Gushee and Glen Stassen (2016) provide a good counter-argument by suggesting that the Sermon on the Mount contains practical guidelines that can transform the lives of his followers. They note: 'Clearly, Jesus's way as taught in the Sermon on the Mount concerns much more than our worship. It concerns sexual relations, marriage, truth telling, loving enemies, and investing our money' (:89).

Jesus' Sermon on the Mount is surely one of the passages of the Bible that is most misunderstood and overlooked. At the same time, it is the most helpful Scripture if one wants to tackle easy believism, cheap grace, prosperity gospel, Charismatic mysticism and Christian nominalism. In other words, Jesus' teachings in this sermon would appear to be much needed in the Rehoboth community today.

## Response to the Sermon on the Mount

Regardless of how one understands inaugurated kingdom eschatology (now and not yet), there is a broad consensus today that being part of God's Kingdom must have ethical implications for every believer in Christ:

> In the end, the transformation associated with the in-breaking of the Kingdom is not merely an abstract exercise in theology or definition. It is designed to impact life. Thus, the connection between Kingdom and living or Kingdom and ethics needs attention [....] Those who are his have acknowledged their need for God and his provision by faith alone. As a result, they have entered into an enduring relationship to God. That relationship entails a call from God on the life of the disciple (Bock 2004)

When we look at the teachings of Jesus as they are recorded in the gospels we notice that they are often accompanied by a call to put them into practice (cf. Bailey 2013:139). In Luke 11:17-26, for example, Jesus is teaching about evil spirits when a woman responds to his teaching and Jesus replies: 'Blessed rather are those who hear the word of God and obey it' (:28). In Matthew 7:24-27 Jesus tells a whole parable, i.e. the parable of the wise and foolish builders, to demonstrate how important it is for his followers to apply his teachings in their lives: 'But everyone who hears these words of mine and does not put them into practice is like a foolish man who built his house on sand. The rain came down, the streams rose, and the winds blew and beat against that house, and it fell with a great crash' (:26-27). In other words, Jesus' teachings are crucial for living the Christian life. Arland Hultgren (2000:136) writes:

> Discipleship that is sound and enduring is the issue addressed in this parable. Such a quality of discipleship is illustrated. The disciple who goes beyond mere lip service to Jesus […] to maturity is one who lives in union with Jesus, listens to him, and practices what he teaches. The parable in context speaks against hypocrisy, but it also exhorts the disciple of Jesus to give care to becoming mature and strong.

However, as Gushee and Stassen (2016:xvi) in their book *Kingdom Ethics* argue, the teachings of Jesus are often ignored not only in churches across the confessional spectrum but also in the theological discipline of Christians ethics. Churches and academics are often guilty of evading Jesus: the one who is the cornerstone of the Christian faith. This would appear to be especially true for his Sermon on the Mount. Gushee and Stassen write: '[T]he teachings and practices of Jesus – especially the largest block of his teachings, the Sermon on the Mount – are routinely ignored or misinterpreted in the preaching and teaching ministry of the churches and in Christian scholarship in ethics.' As a result, the moral beliefs, practices and witness of Christians are affected negatively (:xvi). Instead of doing what Jesus wants them to do, Christians become more susceptible to worldly ideologies.

When we look at modern textbooks on Christian ethics Gushee's and Stassen's criticism seems to be justified. In his book *Exploring Christian Ethics* Kyle Fedler (2006), for example, devotes 155 pages to the biblical foundations of Christian ethics. However, only 35 of these 155 pages deal with the teachings of Jesus. In Robin Lovin's *An Introduction to Christian Ethics,* the author deals with the teachings of Jesus, but they are seen as only one source of many. Lovin (2011:3) writes:

> Christian ethics has its roots in the work of the Hebrew prophets, who called people to renew their covenant with God by living with justice, kindness, and humility. It grows from the teachings of Jesus, who taught love of God and neighbour. Christian ethics is closely connected with another tradition of critical reflection that begins with Greek philosophy and asks what it is that everybody is seeking.

The way scholars understand Jesus' Sermon on the Mount varies. Jürgen Moltmann, for example, views the sermon as a protest against injustice and violence (Agang 2011:171). Moltmann (1993:127) writes: 'Public discussions show that as far as public action is concerned, the centre of the Sermon in the Mount is the liberation from violence; enmity is to be surmounted through the creation of peace. The presupposition here is that humanity's real sin is the violence that leads to death; and that consequently, humanity's salvation is to be in the peace that serves our common life.' Hauerwas seems to share Moltmann's interpretation. He believes that to read the Sermon on the Mount one needs to have a certain conviction: '[Y]ou cannot rightly read the Sermon on the Mount unless you are a pacifist' (quoted in Tolonen 2013:113).

Most scholars agree that Jesus' Sermon on the Mount is concerned with ethics. Some see Matthew 5-7 as an ethical text which helps Christians to make decisions in everyday life. Donald Hagner (1997:45), for example, holds that the Sermon on the Mount is a 'call to Christian Ethics', while Jeremy Holtom (2013:547) writes that the Sermon on the Mount 'presents the reader with a structured series of ethical pronouncements which are delivered directly from the mouth of Jesus.' Charles Talbert (2004), however, argues that the Sermon on the Mount must not be seen and understood as a mere ethical text. It must be seen as a text which addresses not only the horizontal dimension of life but also the vertical dimension, i.e. the believer's relationship with God. He writes:

The teaching of the Sermon on the Mount, like that of biblical law, prophecy and wisdom, cannot be reduced to ethics (the horizontal). In all these
streams of biblical material, the ethical is but one dimension of the larger
concern for "covenant faithfulness", which includes the vertical as well.
The Sermon on the Mount contains material focused on piety as well as that
concerned with ethical behaviour. Is it with ethics that the Sermon is
concerned? Yes and no! Yes, the Sermon is concerned with ethics. No that
is not all about which it is concerned (:46).

Talbert goes on to explain that Jesus' sermon in Matthew 5-7 has the function of a
catalyst for character formation (:46). As such, it is less concerned with the decision
making of Jesus' disciples and more concerned 'with the kind of person the decision
maker is' (:48). To support his view Talbert points to the opening verses 5:3-12, i.e.
the beatitudes: 'The Sermon on the Mount opens with a unit…that includes material
about vertical and horizontal relationships in which disciples find themselves and
that functions in the interests of character formation' (:48). In his commentary on
Matthew Michael Wilkins (2004:198) recognises the vertical and horizontal
dimensions which can be found in Jesus' sermon. Thus, he speaks of the Sermon on
the Mount as a model for discipleship. He writes:

We must see the Sermon as the realistic, though ideal, model of the
Christian life. The SM [Sermon on the Mount] gives the deal of discipleship
[…], yet that goal is set within a realistic understanding of everyday human
life as it will be transformed through participation in the new covenant […]
Although he does not mention the Holy Spirit explicitly in the SM, as the
Spirit-anointed messianic inaugurator of the Kingdom of God […] Jesus
exemplifies the kind of life that is empowered by the Spirit to live out the
radical teaching included in the SM.

Similarly, Troy Troftgruben (2020:234) points out that both dimensions, the vertical
and the horizontal, are not separated from one another. Jesus' sermon presents us
with a vision in which both dimensions are intrinsically linked to each other. He
writes:

It gives us a different vision: one where the more vertical spiritual practices of prayer and fasting support ethical activism, and where the more horizontal practices of justice and neighbor-love support relationship with God. The two are not to be separated easily. Vitality in each area, in fact, depends upon a healthy engagement with the other.

## The Call for Righteousness

Righteousness is an important term in Matthew's Gospel and has a significant implication in the Sermon on the Mount (Przybylski 2004:105ff). Thus, we read the following words of Jesus in Matthew 5:20: 'For I tell you that unless your righteousness surpasses that of the Pharisees and the teachers of the law, you will certainly not enter the kingdom of heaven.' Righteousness is undoubtedly a key term in Jesus' sermon (cf. Kotva 1996:111). Benno Przybylski (2004:116) writes about the meaning of this key term: 'While the Gospel of Matthew clearly indicates that salvation is a gift of God, righteousness is seen only as a demand of God made upon man.' In other words, Jesus intentionally uses the word 'righteousness' in his Sermon on the Mount as an instrument to define the identity of followers. Though righteousness can be used in a soteriological sense, here it is mainly used in an ethical sense. By speaking of righteousness, Jesus refers to the proper behavioural norms and attitudes for his disciples. Hagner (2008:173) comments:

> This community of the kingdom is called to faithfulness to the Torah [...], but, as we will see, in a unique way. Jesus does not call the community to follow the Torah directly, but to follow his teaching [...] For it is the Messiah's teaching that represents the true interpretation of the Torah.

It is noteworthy that the noun *dikaiosune* [righteousness] occurs seven times in Matthew's Gospel, more than in any other writing of the New Testament, except for Romans and 2 Corinthians (cf. Talbert 1992:777). However, some scholars interpret the concept of righteousness in Matthew's Gospel differently. Roland Deines (2008:80-81), for example, argues that the righteousness Jesus speaks about in Matthew 5:20 is not rooted in the Torah but in him. Deines writes: 'I think that it is appropriate to summarize the Matthean concept of righteousness as Jesus-right-eousness. The intention of this phrase is to point out that this righteousness is not possible without Jesus' (:81). The problem with this interpretation is, as Mothy Varkey (2017:101) points out, that 'this does not account for both the programmatic statement in 5:17-19 and the appearance of the Pharisees and scribes in 5:20'.

Hagner (1992:112) says that the evidence for the eschatological interpretation would be that the beatitudes are intended to encourage the downtrodden. Robert Gundry (1982:70) holds that righteousness could refer to God's exercise of justice, which can lead to the eschatological vindication of the poor, meek and persecuted disciples. This interpretation corresponds with the beatitude in Luke 6:21: 'Blessed are you who hunger now, for you will be satisfied.' Warren Carter (2000:134) argues that righteousness refers to God's righteous punishment of a society that exploits the poor and marginalized.

Another interpretation is to understand righteousness as a virtue required from the disciples. In this case, righteousness would refer to the desire to live in full accordance with God's will (Davies & Allison 2004:452; Strecker 1971:156; Turner 2008:151). This interpretation relates to the Jewish sense of the word that implies 'the ideal conduct in adherence to God's ordinances' (Przybylski 2004:35).

The use of the present participles *peinontes* and *difontes* [hunger and thirst] should be noted. It implies that righteousness is something that should continuously be desired: 'Righteousness should ever be sought, must always be a goal which lies ahead: it is never in the grasp' (Davies & Allison 2004:453). Such ethical conduct demonstrates the highest form of true Christian discipleship. Put differently, this beatitude functions as an encouragement to the community to strive towards living according to the standards that Jesus has set. God's will should be done on earth as it is done in heaven (Mt 6:10). There can be very little doubt that the righteousness in Matthew 5:20 refers to ethical conduct.


## Ethical Demands of the Kingdom

What follows in verses 21 to 47 is an explanation of the ethical demands of the Kingdom in relation to the Old Testament. Jesus could not assume that everything his disciples had heard about the Old Testament law was really in the Old Testament (Carson 2001:44). The reason for this was the treatment of particular oral traditions by the Pharisees and teachers of the law who considered them as equal in authority with the books of the Old Testament. After having assured his hearers that he has come to uphold the Old Testament law, Jesus turns to several passages from the law to demonstrate the truth behind them (Kapolyo 2006:1120). In the following, we will briefly look at what Jesus has to say about murder, adultery, oaths and the treatment of enemies.

### *Murder and Reconciliation*

Jesus begins with the fifth commandment 'You shall not murder'.[1] In verses 21 and 22 we read: 'You have heard that it was said to the people long ago, 'Do not murder, and anyone who murders will be subject to judgment.' But I tell you that anyone who is angry with his brother will be subject to judgment.' The Pharisees and experts of the law had come up with a very narrow interpretation of the Old Testament commandment, which Jesus felt needed correction. In their view, they kept the fifth commandment as long as they did not kill anyone physically, as long as they did not spill human blood in homicide (Stott 2000:83). As long as they did not murder a person by strangling, poisoning or stabbing him or her they were not committing any sin, so they thought. The religious leaders had reduced murder to the physical act, and this is apparently what they taught the people. As a result, many people did not have a problem being filled with anger against someone else. Yes, they even thought it was perfectly alright to hate another person. Jesus challenged this attitude. 'He insisted that ethics of His kingdom', as Charles Quarles (2011:108) notes, 'exceeded the standards of the OT, so that even a murderous attitude was deserving of the penalty prescribed for murder.' Jesus makes clear that one can also murder people by using words of contempt and slander; one can even commit murder in one's heart. Anything that violates the dignity and sanctity of a human being qualifies as murder.

---

[1] According to the Lutheran numbering of the Ten Commandments 'You shall not murder' is the fifth commandment, whereas in the Reformed tradition it is the sixth commandment.

G. Campbell Morgan (1954:57) writes the following about Jesus' ethical teaching in these verses and its meaning for Christians:

> Oh this ethic of Jesus, how it scorches! It was so easy a thing to do no murder. Through the accident of birth, or the accident of earlier sur-roundings we are devoid of a certain kind of animal courage, and so do not murder. But oh my soul, when He says if I am angry and contemptuous I am in danger of Gehenna, there is only one thing to do – hurry to the Cross and its blood and its cleansing; to the Resurrection and its life and its dynamic. This ethic of Jesus does not express itself in small rules but in great principles; not in a decalogue on stone, but in a requirement in the heart, is the severest thing that the world has ever had.

Jesus also presents his hearers with an alternative. He tells them to avoid anger and insults at all costs and take action as quickly as possible. To make this point he is using two illustrations here. The first one is taken from going to the temple to offer sacrifices to God and the second one from going to court to answer the charges of an accuser. In both cases, the situation is basically the same: somebody has a grievance against a believer; and in both cases the message is the same: Go and do something about it, seek reconciliation immediately. Green (1988:75) comments: 'Among children of the Kingdom, acceptable worship involves repairing relation-ships. And reconciliation with others flows from reconciliation from God.'

### *Adultery, Lust and Discipline*

Jesus continues with a strong warning against lust and its consequences. In verse 29 we read: 'You have heard that it was said, 'Do not commit adultery.' But I tell you that anyone who looks at a woman lustfully has already committed adultery with her in his heart.' With these words, Jesus again criticises the Pharisees, the religious leaders and their followers who had deliberately distorted the Old Testament law. In this case, it is the sixth commandment which the people of Israel received from God through his prophet Moses: 'Do not commit adultery.'[2] The Pharisees and teachers of the law had limited the scope of this particular commandment. Although the sin of desiring another man's wife is included in the tenth commandment where it says 'You shall not covet your neighbours wife', these religious experts found it more comfortable to ignore this. In their view, they kept the sixth commandment about adultery as long as they avoided the act of adultery itself. As long as they did not sleep with another man's wife they were obedient to God, so they thought. Of course, they would agree that adultery was wrong, but that was easy to agree to, because they had found a way to undermine God's commandment. They had come up with a very narrow interpretation of the commandment. They had found a very narrow definition of sexual sin and a very broad definition of sexual purity, which were both convenient to them.

Jesus, however, makes no such distinction between the physical act of sexual intercourse and the internal lust that may lead to the physical act. He condemns both the outward act of adultery and the inward act of lust (Alvord 2013:129). As a matter of fact, Jesus shifts, as Hagner (1993:121) notes, 'the attention from the external act to the inner thought.' Hagner continues to explain: 'There, in the inner person, lie the real problem and the initial guilt [...] Where lust exists, discipleship of the kingdom requires dramatic and determined action to rid oneself of the cause' (:121). Of course, Jesus' demand to cut off hands and pluck out eyes must not be taken literally. These are deliberate exaggerations (Wright 2002:47). Jesus mentions the hand as the main organ for action and the eye as the main organ for lust (Dray 1998:64). Both organs must be disciplined if one wants to avoid temptation.

### *Oaths and Honesty*

In verse 33 Jesus refers to another popular teaching by saying: 'Again, you have heard that it was said to the people long ago, 'Do not break your oath, but fulfill to

---

[2] According to the Lutheran numbering of the Ten Commandments 'You shall not commit adultery' is the sixth commandment, whereas in the Reformed tradition it is the seventh commandment.

the Lord the vows you have made.' But I tell you, do not swear an oath at all […]'
Andy Angel (2019:56) points out that unlike before, in his teachings on adultery and
murder, Jesus does not refer to any particular Old Testament law here. While
passages such as Leviticus 19:12, Numbers 30:2 and Deuteronomy 23:21 require
people to fulfill vows they have made in the name of the Lord, they do not require
them to make such vows. Consequently, Jesus is not introducing a new rule that
contradicts the Old Testament. He is not forbidding the careful use of vows and
oaths, which we are required to make in certain situations. Instead, he is doing
something much more radical than coming up with a new regulation.

At Jesus's time, people were using oaths and vows as a way of accommodating
to dishonesty in their daily lives. The Pharisees and teachers of the law had twisted
the biblical teaching on taking oaths and making vows. They argued that only an
oath "to the Lord" was absolutely binding (Morris 1995:124). Only when someone
swore and used the name of God he had to stick to the promise or say the truth. Only
when someone swore by God (or towards Jerusalem, by the gold of the temple, or
the offering on the altar) a promise was unbreakable (Kennard 2008:126). In all other
cases, in which God's name was not explicitly used, keeping a vow or oath was not
necessary (Stott 2000:100). Put differently, in all other cases, people were not bound
by their vows. Such 'non-binding oaths included swearing by heaven, by earth, by
Jerusalem, by the temple, by the altar, and by one's own head' (Kennard 2008:126).

The religious leaders had found a kind of loophole that allowed them and others
to make vows without having to keep them, so they thought. In real life, this teaching
led to a ridiculous practice. Whenever people did not have the intention to keep a
promise or say the truth they would avoid God's name and instead swear by heaven,
Jerusalem or the earth (Morris 1995:124). Making vows or taking oaths had become
a means of allowing people to spread lies and half-truths. It gave them the chance to
practise dishonesty in certain situations or areas of their lives.

Jesus, however, makes clear that such a practice is unacceptable for his disciples. He gives two reasons. First, in verse 35 he says, 'But I tell you, do not swear
an oath at all: either by heaven, for it is God's throne; or by the earth, for it is his
footstool; or by Jerusalem, for it is the city of the Great King.' Put differently, even

if people avoid God's name and swear by heaven, the earth, Jerusalem or their own head instead, they actually do not exclude God, because heaven, earth, the city of Jerusalem and even their own heads are all linked with God. They belong to him; they are all part of his creation. Consequently, there is no real difference if someone swears an oath by God or by heaven or by Jerusalem.

Second, for citizens of God's kingdom it is not necessary to swear an oath or make a vow at all before they speak the truth or make a promise. 'All you need to say is simply 'Yes' or 'No'; anything beyond this comes from the evil one', says Jesus. In other words, there is no need for a disciple of Jesus to appeal to the witness of a part of his body or the life of his mother, let alone to God himself, if his or her straightforward 'yes' or 'no' means exactly that, no more and no less.

Christians should not need to make a vow or take an oath to increase the credibility of what they are saying, because they are called to be honest, to speak the truth and to keep what they promise all the time. As followers of Jesus, they need to have a reputation for honesty and reliability. Followers of Jesus should say what they mean and mean what they say. F.F. Bruce (1983:67) states: 'The followers of Jesus should be known as men and women of their word. If they are known to have a scrupulous regard for truth, then what they say will be accepted without the support of any oath.'

### Active Love

Finally, Jesus teaches his audience about love, 'You have heard that is was said, "Love your neighbour and hate your enemy." But I tell you, love your enemies and pray for those who persecute you, that you may be children of your Father in heaven' (:43-45). The word translated love here is *agape*. The words 'love your neighbour' echo Leviticus 19:18, a foundational passage of Jewish ethics (Mounce 1998:49). Most scholars rightly point out that nowhere in the Old Testament can we find the explicit command 'hate your enemy' (e.g. Hagner 1993:134). However, in Leviticus 19:18 the commandment to love one's neighbour applies only to fellow Israelites, 'Do not seek revenge or bear a grudge against anyone among your people, but love your neighbour as yourself.' In addition, several Old Testament verses, such as

Exodus 34:12, Deuteronomy 7:2 or 23:6, call upon the Israelites to oppose their national enemies. Michael Eaton (1999:102) notes:

> The Mosaic law certainly demanded that Canaanites be treated with utmost severity. 'Hate your enemy' is a fair summary of what should be Israel's attitude to the Canaanites, as required by the Mosaic law. First century Jewish teaching no doubt exploited this strand of the law (one thinks of the way the Samaritans were hated), but the law encouraged it in some ways.

Leon Morris (1995:130), who disagrees with this view, points out that the word 'hate' can also be used in the sense of 'love less'. He, therefore, concludes 'that those who summed up Old Testament teaching as calling for love for neighbors and hatred for enemies were oversimplifying' (:130). Anyway, Jesus clearly extends the definition of neighbour as we can it find in Leviticus 19:18. He commands his followers to love all people, including outsiders and those who persecute them. Tom Wright (2002:51) comments:

> Jesus offers *a new sort of justice*, a creative, healing, restoration justice. The old justice found in the Bible was designed to prevent revenge running away with itself. Better an eye for an eye and a tooth for a tooth than an escalating feud with each side going one worse than the other. But Jesus goes on better still. Better to have no vengeance at all, but rather a creative way forward, reflecting the astonishingly patient love of God himself [...]

Based on Matthew 5:21-48, Crook (2016:82) identifies four characteristics of *agape* love. First, agape is the exact opposite of hatred. While the latter is divisive, the former is a unifying force. Second, agape is an active force. It expresses itself in positive ways. Third, agape is impartial in its concern for other people. It does not distinguish between the good and the bad. Fourth, agape is universal, i.e. it loves everyone. 'Jesus concluded this observation', Crook notes, 'by cautioning his disciples to be perfect as God is perfect. The word "perfect" means "complete' or "mature". Jesus' disciples are therefore to be complete in their love, loving all people' (:82).

## Religious Obligations and Ethical Values

In chapter 6, verse 1 Matthew tells us how Jesus picks up the theme of righteousness mentioned before in chapter 5, verse 20, 'but with special application to religious observance rather than to ethical obedience [...] (France 1985:131). The next 17 verses deal with the most prominent religious obligations of Jewish piety, i.e. giving to the needy, prayer and fasting. Robert Mounce explains the main point of Jesus' teaching here: 'The followers of Jesus are to avoid all ostentatious display in order to attract attention to themselves.'

### *Giving to the Needy*

In this part of his Sermon on the Mount Jesus deals with the way people should live in the sight of God. He starts by explaining to them what is expected from members of his kingdom concerning giving to those in need (6:1-4). If we have a closer look at this short passage we will find at least four principles that are relevant for followers of Jesus.

The first principle that we can find here is *giving is not optional*. In verse 2 Jesus says: 'So when you give to the needy' and in verse 3 'But when you give to the needy'. Obviously, Jesus assumes that his disciples give to those who are in need (cf. Hill 1981:132). To Jesus it is clear that his followers will support the poor, and that they will do so generously. Giving to the poor was an important part of Jewish social and religious life. From the days of Moses God had expressed his concern for the needy and the vulnerable. The Old Testament is full of teachings on compassion for the poor (e.g. Exodus 23:10-11; Deuteronomy 14:28-29; Leviticus 23:22). To give money for the poor was one of the most sacred duties among the Jewish people at Jesus' time (cf. Osborne 2010:219), and there is no indication that Jesus wanted his followers to stop giving to the poor. Giving to the poor is a practical way of showing neighbourly love. If we have a closer look at the New Testament we will see that the early church practiced exactly that kind of love. In Acts, chapter 2, for example, Luke describes the life of the first Christian congregation in Jerusalem: 'All the believers were together and had everything in common. Selling their possessions and goods, they gave to anyone as he had need' (:44-45). The Christians in Jerusalem loved God and their fellow believers so much that they freely shared with those who had less.

If we want to give the second principle a title we could call it *disciples of Jesus give with the right motive*. Jesus says in verses 1 and 2: 'Be careful not to practice your righteousness in front of others to be seen by them. If you do, you will have no reward from your Father in heaven. "So when you give to the needy, do not announce it with trumpets, as the hypocrites do in the synagogues and on the streets, to be honored by others.' Obviously, there were people like the Pharisees who were tempted to give to the poor to improve their own reputation. They gave but also made sure that everyone would learn about it. They probably shared it with others in the synagogues and in the streets, both public places where many fellow citizens were gathered. Jesus is using a very vivid picture here; he says that they are spreading the news about their generosity like people who are blowing a trumpet (Osborne 2010:219). Surely there cannot be anything more public than the sounding of a trumpet. To put it differently: These benefactors make a public display of their generosity. Stott (2000:128) comments: 'A ravenous hunger for the praise of men was the besetting sin of the Pharisees [...] So insatiable was their appetite for human commendation that it quite spoiled their giving. Jesus ridicules the way they turned it into a public performance.' The motivation of the Pharisees is not to help the poor. They are not inspired by their gratefulness towards God and what he has done for them. No, they do what they do because they are seeking the praise of their fellow believers. They want to be known as generous, as caring people. But that, says Jesus, is sheer hypocrisy.

The right way of giving, says Jesus, is the way of secrecy. We can find that principle in verse 3: 'But when you give to the needy, do not let your left hand know what your right hand is doing, so that your giving may be in secret.' Jesus assumes that most people use their right hand when they give their money to someone in need, and then he adds that their left hand must not be watching. What does he mean by that? Well, it means two things. Firstly, if you give do not tell anyone else about it. Do not go around and share it with others. That is the obvious meaning: 'all giving must be done in absolute secrecy' (Osborne 2010:220). However, the principle of secrecy goes further than that. Not only should his disciples not tell other people about their giving, no, in a certain sense they are not even to tell themselves. Citizens of God's Kingdom are not to be self-conscious of their giving, because their self-consciousness can easily lead to self-righteousness. What does that mean? It means that deep in their heart they start to dwell on their giving and they begin to congratulate themselves on their giving. But how do disciples give in secrecy then? The secret is probably not to think about donation again, not to keep recalling it.

Such giving, says Jesus will be rewarded. Those who gave money for the poor to improve their reputation have received all the reward they are going to get. They wanted the praise of their fellow believers, they received the praise of their fellow believers. 'Truly I tell you, they have received their reward in full.' Hypocrites like that cannot expect a heavenly reward; they have already been paid in full. There is nothing else to come. But those who give with the right attitude will be rewarded, says Jesus: 'Then your Father, who sees what is done in secret, will reward you.' Scholars disagree over the nature of this reward. Stott's (2000:132) suggestion is quite appealing: 'What, then, is the 'reward', which the heavenly Father gives the secret giver? [...] It is probably the only reward which genuine love wants when making a gift to the needy, namely to see the need relieved.' The greatest reward is to see that the money one gives makes a real difference in the life of a needy person.

### *Prayer*

In verse 6, for example, Jesus criticises those who 'love to pray standing in the synagogues and on the street corner to be seen by others.' A sin that disciples of Jesus need to avoid in prayer is hypocrisy. It is a sin that according to Jesus some people of his time were guilty of. Jesus does not mention their names here but he is likely talking about the Pharisees who were admired for their devotion to the Law of Moses, their knowledge of the Old Testament writings and their disciplined life-style (cf. Stott 2000:133). The Pharisees correctly believed that prayer was very important. As devout Jews they prayed three times a day, usually standing but sometimes also kneeling (cf. Kapolyo 2006:1122). They prayed in the synagogues and they even prayed in the streets, and there was nothing wrong with that (Mounce

1998:54-55). However, what was wrong was their motive for doing so. They prayed not because they loved prayer so much or the God they were supposed to be praying to.

Jesus had uncovered their true motive for standing in the synagogue or in the streets with their hands uplifted to heaven: they wanted to be seen by others (Osborne 2010:225). They wanted others to see how pious and devoted they were. What they really wanted was applause and admiration from their fellow believers. The Pharisees were not driven by the desire to speak to God, but by their pride; they first and foremost loved themselves and the opportunity to parade themselves. When the Pharisees raised their hands in prayer people around them stood still and looked at them with admiration. When they moved their lips people were touched with awe. The Pharisees played to their audience (Cf. Carson 2001:64). And that, says Jesus, is sheer hypocrisy. Hypocrites like that, says Jesus, 'have received their reward in full' (6:5).

## Loyalty to Kingdom Values

While the first part of Matthew chapter 6 mainly deals with hypocrisy and tends to be rather negative in tone, the second part is much more positive as Jesus demands 'unswerving loyalty to kingdom values' (Carson 2001:82, 89).

Verses 19 to 24 are all about money and material wealth. Jesus does not condemn earthly treasures but he warns his disciples, as Kapolyo (2006:1123) notes, 'to cultivate a healthy detachment from the lure of wealth.' In contrast to heavenly treasures, earthly wealth is perishable. It can be lost in many different ways. Therefore, Jesus' followers should seek treasures in heaven that cannot be destroyed. They gain these heavenly treasures by obeying God in all areas of their lives. The kinds of treasure people store up for themselves tell us much about their spiritual condition, 'For where your treasure is, there your heart will also be', says Jesus (:21). Disciples of Jesus cannot be truly devoted to God if they are devoted to money and all the things money can buy (Green 1988:84). Thus, we read in verse 24: 'No one can serve two masters. Either you will hate the one and love the other, or you will be devoted to the one and despise the other. You cannot serve both God and Money.' Love of money, which the apostle Paul calls the root of all evil (1 Tim 6:10), and true love for God are mutually exclusive. They are, as Michael Green (1988:84) writes, 'rival affections'. Money and all property and wealth are by nature 'neutral'. Disciples of Jesus can use them to serve God, but money and material things can also claim their devotion (France 1985:139), or as Kapolyo (2006:1123) helpfully comments: 'Money should be our servant in the service of God, not a god to which we owe allegiance as slaves.'

Jesus leaves us with no doubt here that his disciples cannot serve God with half their being and money with the other half. They can only serve one master, and anyone who has divided his allegiance between God and money has actually given it to money. With two masters one cannot give total allegiance to one (cf. Osborne 2010:244). Disciples who try to share God with other loyalties commit idolatry. Consequently, they should not worry about material things.

In verses 25 to 34, Jesus not only explains why worrying is wrong but also gives an antidote to it. Three times Jesus is asking his disciples not to worry in this short passage. Twice he is asking them specifically not to worry about food or clothes, and one time he is asking them more generally not to worry about the immediate future. 'Worry is essentially a failure to trust God' (Green 1988:85) As a matter of fact worry is a sign of unbelief, it is practical atheism. Jesus calls his disciples 'you of little faith' (:30). By telling them not to worry Jesus is asking them to put their trust in God, and he gives them a good reason to do so, 'Look at the birds of the air; they do not sow or reap or store away in barns, and yet your heavenly Father feeds them. Are you not much more valuable than they? (:26)' God sees that even the birds are fed. However, children of God are much more precious to God than birds. Therefore there is no need for them to worry. They can trust God that he will look after them. The same message can be found in a second illustration that Jesus uses in verses 28 to 29: 'See how the flowers of the field grow. They do not labor or spin. Yet I tell you that not even Solomon in all his splendor was dressed like one of these.'

# CHAPTER THREE
## Survey among Church Leaders in Rehoboth

A quantitative questionnaire on the understanding of the Kingdom of God and its ethical implications was distributed among ordained church leaders in the Namibian town of Rehoboth. The church leaders belonged to both mainline Protestant churches and Pentecostal churches. The questionnaire was sent to 40 church leaders. Seventeen of these questionnaires were filled in and were returned to the researcher, which equals a response rate of 43%. An analysis of the questionnaires has led to the following results.

### Social Challenges in Rehoboth

When asked to name the three most significant social challenges which can be observed in the Rehoboth community the church leaders identified drug and alcohol misuse as the biggest challenge. Thus, drug and alcohol abuse was mentioned seventeen times (= 100% of all answers). Other challenges that also fall into the category of individual ethics and which were mentioned by the interviewees are gender-based violence (five times), adultery and sexual immorality (five times), teenage pregnancies (three times), and a high divorce rate (two times). However, the interviewees also named issues that do not fall into the category of individual ethics. Among those issues are poverty (eight times) and unemployment (five times).

These results show that the church leaders are very much aware of the social challenges which the people in Rehoboth are facing. The *Safety and Audit Report Rehoboth* published by The Urban Trust of Namibia (UTN) in 2013, for example, states the following:

> Rehoboth, a town 85 km outside of Windhoek, presents as one of the areas reflecting one of the highest violent crime rates in Namibia. Both police statistics and victimisation data reflect assaults and robberies to be the most common crimes, with between three and four murders monthly [....] Substance abuse is reportedly common, and viewed as one of the major

challenges facing the community, by both the police and community members themselves. Unemployment rates sits at just under one in five, with the rate almost double for young people aged 18 to 20 years.

Many of the views expressed by the interviewees are also shared by a prominent non-Protestant church leader in Rehoboth. In an interview for the *New Era* published in July 2016 Father Chris Jonkers (quoted by New Era Staff Reporter 2016) of the Roman Catholic Church said the following about the problems within the Rehoboth community:

> Unemployment is the root cause of many problems in Rehoboth and Namibian society as a whole, as it exacerbates problems when members of the youth find themselves with limited opportunity. Community programmes are needed to keep the youth busy. Many Grade 10 and 12 dropouts have so much potential and skill, yet they lack a certificate to gain employment. As there are no recreational facilities in Rehoboth, many youth fill their time frequenting shebeens and clubs, where they abuse alcohol and drugs which then spirals into a community with violence, crime and poverty.

## The Challenges of a Christian Lifestyle

Being asked about the way Christians should live, the majority of the interviewees (fifteen out of seventeen) responded that Christians should have a lifestyle that is visibly different from the lifestyle of non-believers. Thus, fifteen respondents say that they agree with the statement that according to Jesus' teaching Christians as citizens of God's kingdom are to be entirely different from non-Christians. Two respondents disagree with this statement. Sixteen interviewees agree with the statement that '[t]he lifestyles of many church members in Rehoboth do not reflect the *ethical* standards which are set by the teachings of the Bible'. Only one interviewee disagrees with this statement. In other words, there is wide agreement among the church leaders that there is a problem in the Christian community in Rehoboth concerning people's lifestyles. The church leaders hold that there is a large number of Christians in Rehoboth who do not live according to the ethical standards which can be found in the Bible. However, there is a variety of views among the church leaders regarding the extent of this challenge. When asked about the percentage of Christians in Rehoboth that live out kingdom ethics the interviewees gave the following answers: 5% (two times), 15% (one time), 20% (one time), 30% (one time); 35% (two times), 40% (two times), 50% (two times) 60% (three times). Three respondents did not give any answer. Put differently, two interviewees have an extremely negative view. They believe that 95% of Rehoboth Christians do not live out kingdom ethics. Eleven respondents hold that half or more of the Christians in Rehoboth fall into this category. Only three interviewees believe that the number of those who do not live out kingdom ethics is smaller than the number of those who do. However, these three respondents believe that the number of those who do not comply with the ethical standards of God's Kingdom is still relatively large, i.e. 40% of the Christian population.

## Preaching on Ethical Issues and Jesus' Sermon on the Mount

All interviewees say that preaching on ethical issues can transform the lives of Christians in Rehoboth. However, when asked to name three biblical passages that they would choose for a sermon on ethical issues eight of seventeen interviewees did not list any passage. Of the nine respondents who gave passages only four mentioned passages from Jesus' Sermon on the Mount. Altogether, eight times passages from Jesus' Sermon on the Mount were chosen (= 30% of passages named). Six times passages were chosen from the Pauline letters or other passages from the Synoptic Gospels respectively (= 56% of passages named). These figures seem to suggest that Jesus' Sermon on the Mount is not regarded by all Rehoboth church leaders as a crucial text for *ethical preaching*. Further analysis of other responses points in the same direction.

Interestingly, fifteen out of the seventeen leaders agree that in his Sermon on the Mount Jesus deals with many ethical issues that are relevant for the community in Rehoboth at large. Adultery and poverty in Spirit are mentioned four times by the interviewees. Jesus' call to be peacemakers, his call to be merciful, and his call to be non-judgmental are mentioned twice. Two interviewees also list Jesus' teaching on divorce. One leader mentions hypocrisy. The church leaders believe that for the members of their churches similar issues, which are addressed by Jesus, are relevant. Three mention the need to be peacemakers while poverty in Spirit, hunger and thirst for righteousness, materialism and purity of heart are mentioned twice each. One interviewee stresses the importance of the ethical standards of Jesus' Sermon on the Mount when he writes: 'Mt. 5:17. The Church must be light and we really do that by following His rule. By restoring love and hope we bring healing for all sorts of social ills.' Three interviewees believe that Jesus' command to love one's enemies (Matthew 5:43-48) is the most important ethical principle which can be found in the Sermon on the Mount.

When being asked to address one particular ethical issue in their next sermon six church leaders, i.e. 38%, would preach on the sin of materialism while two would preach on greed. Five interviewees would preach on poverty. Two would choose to tackle the problem of a judgmental spirit. One leader would preach on the issue of divorce.

The response of the church leaders shows that many issues that are addressed by Jesus in his Sermon on the Mount are very relevant for Christians in Rehoboth today. It seems that a significant number of Rehoboth Christians are struggling with several sins which Jesus deals with in his sermon. They seem, for example, to be preoccupied with possession and wealth and demonstrate a desire to have more and more. There seems to be a tendency to criticise and condemn other people, too. At the same time, there are a larger number of church members who are affected by material poverty. However, Jesus' Sermon on the Mount does not seem to be a natural text for church leaders to choose for a sermon in which they address these issues.

## Jesus and the Kingdom of God

The interviewees were asked about the heart of Jesus' teachings. All interviewees agree that the heart of Jesus' teachings centres around the Kingdom of God and not the Church. The majority of them (eleven interviewees) hold that the expressions *Kingdom of God* and *Kingdom of heaven* are synonyms. Four church leaders (24%), however, believe that the two terms refer to two different realities. One of them explains what he or she means by that. According to him or her, the expression *Kingdom of God* refers to a present reality while the phrase *Kingdom of heaven* refers to a future reality. We have seen before that the majority of scholars disagree with such a view. Robert Stein (1994:61), for example, argues there is plenty of evidence that both terms refer to the same entity. He points out that 'Matthew frequently uses the expression "kingdom of heaven" in the very same saying in which Mark or Luke both use "Kingdom of God" (:61).' Stein continues to say that Matthew also uses both phrases interchangeably (:62). In 19:23-24, Matthew records the following words of Jesus: 'I tell you the truth, it is hard for a rich man to enter the kingdom of heaven. Again I tell you, it is easier for a camel to go through the eye of a needle than for a rich man to enter the Kingdom of God.'

## The Rule of God

The interviewees were also asked to define the Kingdom of God. Eleven interviewees (64%) agree that the basic meaning of the Kingdom of God is 'the rule of God'. Three leaders (18%) hold that the Kingdom of God is identical with the 'Church of God', whereas three other leaders think that the kingdom is to be understood in geographical terms, i.e. that it describes 'the territory of God'.

An analysis of the definitions of the kingdom which the interviewees were asked to give shows that the kingdom as the 'rule of God' is understood in slightly different ways. For one leader the Kingdom of God 'is the place where God rules supreme. It is both present and expectant'. Another understands the rule of God as 'the rule of an eternal, sovereign God over the universe.' Similarly, one defines the kingdom as '[the] mysterious kingly rule of God that transcends time and space'. He or she goes on to say that 'the church testifies or witnesses to that reality because the Church is the primary instrument He [God] uses.' This latter aspect is emphasised by another interviewee who defines the kingdom in the following way:

> The Kingdom of God begins with the true Christian. Preaching the word of
> God and see to, that the Light of His word reflects in all Christians every

day. As we are followers we must lead by example so that the Kingdom of God can be visible in us and God be glorified through us.

While this definition focuses on the present rule of God in the lives of believers another interviewee stresses both the present and future aspect of God's rule over everything:

The Kingdom of God must be seen as a sovereign God who rules the earth, and not only the earth but the whole universe. He is the Lord of creation because creation belongs to him. He is the eternal one…But also, in the future the kingdom will be reinstituted at the second coming of Christ.

However, the same interviewee also speaks of a spiritual rule of God in the lives of Christians: 'The Kingdom of God can also be seen as a spiritual rule over people; those who have given their lives to him and his authority. People who have submitted themselves [to him].' A similar differentiation can be found in the answer of another interviewee. He or she argues that the kingdom is God's spiritual rule in the life of believers: 'Kingdom refers to the reign of God in one's life after repentance and acceptance of Jesus Christ as personal saviour and Lord of my life.' He or she then adds that there is also a 'physical', future dimension of the kingdom: 'It refers to the establishment of a Kingdom in future where God reigns over the cosmos (heaven and earth – the universe) he created, where everything including nature, humankind, animal life, all creatures are under supreme Rule of God'.

## Eschatology

The interviewees were also asked about their eschatological beliefs. Fifteen out of seventeen interviewees (88%) say that they agree with the following statement: 'We are living in an age when the Kingdom of God is already here but not fully here.' Only one interviewee says that he or she does not agree with this statement. One interviewee did not answer the question. In other words, the large majority of church leaders seem to subscribe to the position which is known as inaugurated eschatology. The above-mentioned analysis of their definitions of the Kingdom of God seems to support this conclusion. The advocates of inaugurated eschatology hold that the

Kingdom of God is both present and future. The most prominent of these advocates of the 'already but not yet' view is again Ladd. Laurie Matthias (2015:14-15) describes Ladd's position very well when he writes:

> With careful examination of every reference to the Kingdom of God in the New Testament, he [Ladd] provides evidence that Kingdom of God has already come. As believers in Christ, we have been rescued from the kingdom of darkness and brought into the kingdom of the Son (Col 1:13; Luke 16:16). Thus, the Kingdom of God is within us (Luke 17:20-1); providing us righteousness, peace, and joy in the Holy Spirit (Rom 14:17); and functioning as a mustard seed or yeast in the way it grows in us in our world (Luke 13:18-21). And yet, as Ladd explains, there is also evidence in Scripture that the Kingdom of God has not yet come. Jesus stated that his kingdom was not yet of this world (John 18:36). At some time in the future, those who have put their faith in the redemptive work of Christ on the cross will be welcomed into the Kingdom of God (Matt 25:34; 13:41-3; 8:11, 2 Pet 2:11).

## Kingdom, Church and Mission

Being asked if it is the task of God or the task of the Church to establish the Kingdom of God eight interviewees (47%) say that it is the church's task while five interviewees hold that it is God's task. One leader believes that it is both God's and the Church's task to establish the kingdom. Three interviewees did not answer the question.

It seems that almost half of the interviewees lean towards the concept of king-dom mission, which stresses that it is the Church's mission to build or extend God's kingdom. To support this view the following arguments were typically presented: (a) The Kingdom of God/kingdom of heaven is the central theme in Jesus' teaching; (b) For his disciples who follow him Jesus is their role model in mission. Consequently, the Church's mission should be concerned about God's kingdom. McKnight (2014:57) writes the following about kingdom mission: 'Kingdom mission is the way of engagement, integration, incarnation, involvement and participation. It is the way of Jesus, the way of "neighboring", and the way of living in the world without being of the world.' However, this view has been challenged by other authors. They stress that Jesus will bring his kingdom and so he teaches his disciples in Matthew 6:10 to pray 'your kingdom come'. Frankie Phillips (2013:14), for example, writes:

> Believers are misguided into accepting the notion that in some way we are to establish Christ's Kingdom for Him, so that He can come to rule over it. He does not want any part of this world, no matter how we might be able to fix it up. His Kingdom will not be a "fix-it-up" project. The Bible teaches that He will build his church and perfect it, destroy the kingdoms of the world, and establish a new order for the redeemed race that will live with Him and share rulership of His Kingdom.

# CHAPTER FOUR
## Conclusion and Suggestions

### The Need for Preaching on Ethical Issues

The survey shows that the Christian leaders in Rehoboth are very much aware of the social and ethical problems which the Rehoboth community is facing. The church leaders also agree that there is a large number of Christians in Rehoboth whose lifestyles are not in line with the ethical standards which can be found in the Bible. In other words, the research results seem to confirm the hypothesis that there is a discrepancy between Jesus' teaching in the Sermon on the Mount, which forms the centre of his ethical teachings, and the attitude and behaviour of Christians which can be observed in Rehoboth.

While the church leaders say that preaching and teaching on ethical issues is important to change the situation in Rehoboth for the better, the research shows that the majority of them do not consider Jesus' Sermon on the Mount as an important basis for such preaching and teaching. Furthermore, all leaders think that the heart of Jesus' teachings centres on God's kingdom and not the Church. However, this conviction does not seem to have much influence on the selection of their sermon passages. It is also striking that half of the leaders did not name any biblical passages which they would choose for a sermon on ethical issues. In summary, it seems that for a significant number of leaders preaching on ethical issues does not play an important role in practice, though, in theory, they acknowledge such a need.

Against this background, it is not surprising that the witness of the church in Rehoboth is not as effective as it could be. In his book *Foundations for the Flock* Conrad Mbewe (2011:135-136) a Zambian Baptist theologian, helpfully highlights the relationship between practical Christian preaching and the witness of trans-formed Christian lives in the community. Mbewe writes:

> One of the reasons why Paul was concerned for applicatory preaching was
> because he knew that the church was to be salt and light in the world –

especially through the lives of its members [...] As a pastor you must never be content with Christianity from your people that ends in the church building. Aim for transformed lives that affect the way in which people live in their homes, work places, schools and society.

It is not clear from the research if this hesitation to teach biblical ethical standards is related to the leaders' views of God's kingdom, as claimed by our working hypothesis. A strictly futurist or premillennial interpretation of the kingdom which tends to see 'the kingdom as coming primarily or exclusively by God's action and cataclysmically rather than gradually' (Snyder 2001:102), could explain such a lack of teaching in the churches. However, most of the Rehoboth church leaders seem to be adherents of an inaugurated eschatology. Apart from that, their other views regarding the Kingdom of God differ quite significantly. Thus, one-third of the leaders reject the view which first and foremost equates the Kingdom of God with the rule of God. Furthermore, a quarter of the leaders hold that the terms 'kingdom of God' and 'kingdom of heaven' refer to two different entities. Finally, there is no agreement among the leaders on the question if it is God's task or the Church's task to establish God's Kingdom.

However, what the research also shows is that there are church leaders in Rehoboth who hold views regarding the Kingdom of God which are contrary to modern scholarship. Among these views is the idea that the Kingdom of God is identical with the Church of God or the view that the Kingdom of God is to be understood as Rehoboth. Based on my research I would like to offer the following suggestions and recommendations.

## Providing Teaching on God's Kingdom

First, there is a need for a better understanding of God's Kingdom among Rehoboth church leaders. To encourage church leaders and church members to share their views of the kingdom and to learn from the Bible and scholarship, the Rehoboth Pastors' Fraternal should organise a series of meetings that take place in different churches.

## Encouraging Sermons on Jesus' Sermon on the Mount

Second, there is obviously a need for more ethical teaching and preaching in the churches in Rehoboth. To encourage Rehoboth church leaders to preach more on ethical issues, the Rehoboth Pastors' Fraternal could organise a preaching workshop which has its focus on Jesus' Sermon on the Mount. Such a workshop could be facilitated by faculty members of one of the theological seminaries in Namibia. Furthermore, there is helpful literature available on the subject. Thus, Billy E. Simmons (1992:125-126), for example, makes the following suggestions for a preaching programme on the Sermon on the Mount:

> If the preceding does not suit your style, you may want to begin the series with an overview sermon. This would take into account the various emphases found throughout the sermon. Some of these are: (1) qualifications for kingdom persons, (2) duties of kingdom persons, and (3) warnings to kingdom persons. Another way to view the entire sermon would be to examine the general theme of righteousness and the various contrasts and comparisons that are found throughout the sermon dealing with this theme. Another approach for an overview sermon might contain the following points: (1) an invitation to the kingdom, (2) requirements for kingdom people, and (3) warnings to those in the kingdom. If you plan to spend one month on the series, you might plan an overview sermon and then divide the material into three other sermons: The Ideal Christian Life, 5:3-16; The Characteristics of the Christian Life, 5:17-7:12; and An Exhortation to Righteous Living, 7:13-27.

Of course, any preaching on Jesus' Sermon on the Mount needs to be contextual.

### Contextual Preaching: Adultery and Gender-Based Violence

Adultery, sexual and gender-based violence are rampant in Rehoboth and throughout Namibia. There has been a steady increase in crimes, such as rape, grievous bodily harm and even murder. Tess Gellert (2020) writes:

> Sexual gender-based violence has been a serious issue in Namibia – specifically intimate-partner violence against women and girls, sexual

violence by non-partners, and femicide […] reports from earlier this year stated that police were receiving at least 200 cases of domestic *violence* every month, and more than 1,600 cases of rape were reported during an 18-month period ending in June 2020. Additionally, lockdowns and stay at home orders put in place to curb the ongoing coronavirus pandemic has made life especially difficult for victims of domestic violence who have been forced to self-isolate with their abusers.

In our honour-shame culture many Namibians, especially men, seem to think that they can get away with their sinful conduct as long as they manage to keep it secret. As long as the community does not know they are doing nothing wrong, so they think. People who think like that need to be reminded that they cannot hide anything, including their sexual immorality and crimes, from God (cf. Ephesians 6:9-10) and 'that anyone who looks at a woman lustfully has already committed adultery with her in his heart.' (Matthew 5:28). With these words Jesus broke the silence and the church needs to do the same today. Isabel Apawo Phiri (2006:3939) states:

> Silence encourages rape, and so the church needs to break its silence by preaching constantly against the abuse of women and children. We need to declare the church and our homes to be zero tolerance zones for any form of sexual abuse.

At Jesus' time, the religious leaders reduced adultery and lust to the sexual act, but Jesus taught differently. He goes beyond the customary views on adultery and lust by affirming that the true meaning of the sixth commandment is much wider than a mere prohibition of acts of sexual immorality. Jesus makes clear that the prohibition of adultery includes the deliberate lustful look and imagination, it includes the lustful attitude. Jesus challenges not only people's beliefs on adultery but also their hearts. Many Namibian Christians today profess to agree with God's commandment but they do not obey it. They are quick to condemn sexual immoral acts and crimes but that does not keep them from fostering their lust by erotic books, DVDs or websites. They forget that pornography is also a form of adultery.

Violence is the use of force to hurt someone else. 'People are subjected to violence whenever they are treated in a way that denies them justice, equality, freedom and human dignity' (Turaki 2006:1043). It often has its roots not only in greed but also in sexism, tribalism and religious prejudice (:1043). Jesus leaves us with no doubt that he abhors that kind of violence, whether physical or emotional. In his Sermon on the Mount, he declares a special blessing on those who bring an end to violence. Thus, he says 'Blessed are the peacemakers, for they will be called the children of God' (Matthew 5:9). Jesus' call to refrain from violence is repeated by the apostle Paul when he writes; 'Do not repay anyone evil for evil' (Romans 12:17). In his story of the Good Samaritan Jesus reminds us that as citizens of his kingdom we have a responsibility for those who have become victims of violence. The Samaritan looks after a man who has been attacked by robbers: 'He went to him and bandaged his wounds, pouring on oil and wine. He put the man on his own donkey, brought him to an inn and took care of him' (Luke 10:34).

### *Contextual Preaching: Poverty*

Namibia is a country in which almost 30% of the population are classified as poor, 15% even as severely poor (National Planning Commission undated:4). In 2017 the World Bank (2017:1) reported the following about poverty in Namibia:

> Despite the progress, daunting challenges for poverty and inequality reduction remain. The economy's steady growth has not generated enough jobs, resulting in sluggish reductions in poverty, inequality, and unemployment. Though falling, poverty rates are relatively high for an upper middle income country. World Bank calculations show that 16.9 percent of the population lived on less than $1.90 a day in 2015. Inequality is among the highest in the world.

How do we as Christians respond to that situation? In his Sermon on the Mount Jesus says 'So when you give to the needy' (5:2). There can be no doubt that he expects us to support those in need. At a later point, Jesus told his disciples not only to love the Lord with all their heart, soul and mind but he also said to them 'Love your neighbour as yourself' (Matthew 22:37-39). Giving to the poor is surely a practical way of showing such kind of neighbourly love. Tim Chester (2004:21) writes: 'The appropriate response to the God who upholds the poor is for us likewise to uphold the cause of the poor. This is the truly religious activity of those who follow the God of the Bible.' A closer look at the New Testament shows us that the early church practiced exactly that kind of neighbourly love. The apostle Paul writes in Galatians chapter 2, verse 10, 'All they asked was that we should continue to remember the poor, the very thing I was eager to do.', and in his first letter, chapter 3, verse 16, John reminds his readers and us: 'If anyone has material possessions and sees his brother in need but has no pity on him, how can the love of God be in him?' Similarly, James warns his first readers and us today that faith in Christ without good deeds is useless: 'Suppose a brother or a sister is without clothes and daily food. If one of you says to them, 'Go in peace, keep warm and well fed, but does nothing about their physical needs, what good is it? In the same way, faith by itself, if it is not accompanied by action, is dead.' (2:15-17).

As Christians, we should support the poor and needy in our communities. We should do it generously, joyfully and with thankful hearts. How can we not give to the poor if God gave for us what is most precious to him: his one and only Son Jesus Christ. How can we who have received God's forgiveness, and mercy, be so heartless now and not share our money and material possessions with those who are suffering? As citizens of God's Kingdom we need to keep an eternal perspective. Christians are to build treasures in heaven 'where moths and vermin do not destroy, and where thieves do not break in and steal' (Matthew 6:20). For where their treasure is, there their heart will be also (:20).

### *Contextual Preaching: Dishonesty and Corruption*

For a long time, Namibia praised itself for being one of the least corrupt countries in Africa. However, this reputation has been shattered in recent years. High ranking politicians have been charged and sentenced for receiving bribe payments or granting favours to family and clan members (cf. Henley 2019). The problem with fovouritism is that it can easily become corruption, as Soro Soungalo (2006:1511) notes: 'A favour may be given in exchange for a bribe of money or some other commodity. In this case, favouritism is not just a speck in someone's eye, but a plank (see Matt. 7:3-5).' He continues:

The fight against favouritism is a major challenge for Christians who are in positions where it is always present. They should make a special effort to live as Christians, in a way that is different from those around them, because they are called to be the light of the world and the salt of the earth (Matt. 5:13-16). But what can be done if the salt has lost its saltiness? (:1511)

Dishonesty has become part of everyday life in Namibia. 'Sorry, I can't help you now. But I will call you back'? is a response Namibians are very familiar with. In most cases 'I will call you back' means that one will never hear from that person again. 'I will call you back is Namlish (Namibian English) for 'I'm not bothered'. Jesus challenges such dishonesty, 'All you need to say is simply "Yes", or "No"; anything beyond this comes from the evil one' (Matthew 5:37). As followers of Jesus, Namibian Christians should never underestimate the power of dishonesty. Dishonesty helps to keep a society in perpetual doubt, distrust, resentment and corruption. A society where people cannot trust each other anymore has no future. Dishonesty is a destructive force.

### Contextual Preaching: Tribalism

Over thirty years after the end of the oppressive and racist apartheid system, tribalism and ethnic divisions can still be observed in Namibia. In an article for *The Namibian* Pius Dunaiski (2020) wrote the following in September 2020:

> Namibia is on a knife's edge and it is increasingly difficult not to sound alarmist and emotional. An honest audit will provide a strong dose of reality on just how unequal the country is along tribal lines. I don't believe it is a mere perception among minorities [...] Right now, we need a majority from all tribes to strongly advocate that Namibia, at all costs, pursue the ideal which prescribes that Namibia belongs to all people – irrespective of their ethnic, racial, gender or religious background. Tribal apologists must be unmasked. Minorities should feel Namibia is also their country. A true sense of ownership is wanting.

Belonging to a tribe or clan can offer many benefits, such as practical support, financial help or protection, to people. However, as Rubin Poshor (2006:316) points out protection and support are distorted when people use them to show favouritism to those who belong to their tribe, despise other ethnic groups or even use violence against them. Unfortunately, many Namibian churches and denominations are still organised along *ethnic / tribal* lines and not always is the relationship between these ecclesiastical bodies a positive one.

In his Sermon on the Mount Jesus stresses that he expects his followers to show a different attitude, 'If you love those who love you, what reward will you get? Are not even the tax collectors doing that? And if you greet only your own people, what are you doing more than others? Do not even pagans do that?' (Matthew 5:46-47). Citizens of God's Kingdom need to learn to show love to all people in Namibia, whatever their ethnic, religious or social background. Likewise, Namibian churches need to curb the scourge of theological and denominational tribalism and seek reconciliation and cooperation with those who belong to a different church tradition.

## Outlook

My study did not seek to answer the question why there is relatively little preaching on ethical issues and particularly teaching and preaching from Jesus' Sermon on the Mount in the churches of Rehoboth. However, I have found that this deficiency is caused by particular theological views of God's Kingdom. It would be helpful to look at that question in depth again and to include the ethical teachings that we can find in the New Testament epistles.

# BIBLIOGRAPHY

Adams, S.A. 2013. *The Genre of Acts and Collected Biography*. Cambridge: Cambridge University Press.

Aging, S.B. 2011. *The Impact of Ethnic, Political, and Religious Violence on Northern Nigeria, and a Theological Reflection on Its Healing*. Carlisle: Langham Partnership.

Angel, A. 2019. *The Jesus You Really Didn't Know: Rediscovering the Teaching Ministry of Jesus*. Eugene: Cascade Books.

Arias, M. 1984. *Announcing the Reign of God: Evangelisation and the Subversive Memory of Jesus*. Philadelphia: Fortress Press.

Bailey, J.L. 2013. *Contrast Community: Practicing the Sermon on the Mount*. Eugene: Wipf & Stock.

Barclay, W. 1999. *The Parables of Jesus*. Louisville: Westminster John Knox Press.

Beasley-Murray, G. 1989. 'Matthew 6:33: The Kingdom of God and the Ethics of Jesus. 'Seek First His Kingdom and Righteousness, and All These Things Will Be Added to You', in *Neues Testament und Ethik: Für Rudolf Schnackenburg*. Merklein, H. (ed). Freiburg: Herder.

Beasley-Murray, G. 1992. *The Kingdom of God in the Teaching of Jesus*. Portland: Tren.

Bickel, D.R. 2001. 'What Does it Mean to Seek the Kingdom of God. Matthew 6:33 and Luke12:31 in the Contexts of the Sermon on the Mount and the Lucan Parables.' <http://citeseerx.ist.psu.edu/viewdoc/summary?doi=10.1.1.607.7523>; date of access: 11.12.2020.

Bock, D.L. 2004. 'The Kingdom of God in New Testament Theology: The Battle, The Christ, The Spirit-Bearer, and Returning Son of Man'. <bible.org/article/kingdom-god-new-testament-theology-battle-christ-spirit-bearer-returning-son-man>; date of access: 11.12.2020.

Bruce, F.F. 1983. *The Hard Sayings of Jesus*. Downers Grove: IVP.

Bruner, F.D. 2004. *Matthew: A Commentary*. Grand Rapids: Eerdmans.

Bryman, A. 2012. *Social Research Methods*. Oxford: Oxford University Press.

Buchanan, G.W. 2005. *The Book of Revelation: Its Introduction and Prophecy*. Eugene: Wipf & Stock.

Buttrick, D. 1998. *Preaching the New and the Now*. Louisville: Westminster John Knox Press.

Buys, G.L. &, Nambala, S.V.V. 2003. *History of the Church in Namibia 1805-1990: An Introduction*. Windhoek: Gamsberg Macmillan.

Carson, D.A. 1996. *The Gagging of God: Christianity Confronts Pluralism*. Grand
  Rapids: Zondervan.

Carson, D.A. 2001. *The Sermon on the Mount: An Evangelical Exposition of Matthew
  5-7*. Carlisle: Paternoster Press.

Carson, D.A. 2017. *Matthew*. Grand Rapids: Zondervan.

Carter, W. 2000. *What Are They Saying about Matthew's Sermon on the Mount*. New
  York: Paulist Press.

Charles, J.D. 2004. '"Do Not Suppose That I have Come": The Ethic of the Sermon on
  the Mount Reconsidered'. *Southwestern Journal of Theology* 46(3):47-70.

Chester, T. 2004. *Good News to the Poor: Sharing he Gospel through Social
  Involvement*. Leicester: IVP.

Clarke, A.B. & Linzey, A. 2006. *Dictionary of Ethics, Theology and Soci*ety. Abingdon:
  Routledge.

Cole, V.B. 2006. 'Mark', in *Africa Bible Commentary*. Adeyemo, T. (ed). Grand Rapids:
  Zondervan.

Collins, R. 2013. *Introduction to the New Testament*. New York: Image.

Colson, C. 1987. *Kingdoms in Conflict*. Grand Rapids: Zondervan.

Crook, R.H. 2016. *An Introduction to Christian Ethics*. Abingdon: Routledge.

Cubillos, R.H. 2017. *Faith, Hope and Love in the Kingdom of God*. Eugene: Pickwick
  Publications.

Davies, W.D. & Allison, D.C. 2004. *A Critical and Exegetical Commentary on the
  Gospel According to Saint Matthew*. London: T & T Clark.

Deines, R. 2008, 'Not the Law but the Messiah: Law and Righteousness in the Gospel of
  Matthew: An Ongoing Debate', in *Upon the Rock: Studies in the Gospel of
  Matthew*. Gurtner, D.M. & Nolland, J. (eds). Grand Rapids: Eerdmans.

Dray, S. 1998. *Matthew's Gospel: Crossway Bible Guide*. Leicester: Crossway Books.

Dunaiski, P. 2020. 'Tribalism and Namibia'. *The Namibian* 18.09.2020.
  <namibian.com.na/204613/archive-read/Tribalism-and-Namibia>; date of
  access: 12.12.2020.

Eaton, M. 1999. *The Way That Leads to life: The Radical Challenge to the Church of the
  Sermon on the Mount*. Fearn: Christian Focus.

Fedler, K.D. 2006. *Exploring Christians Ethics: Biblical Foundations for Morality*.
  Louisville: Westminster John Knox Press.

France, R.T. 1985. *Tyndale New Testament Commentaries: Matthew*. Grand Rapids:
  Eerdmans.

France, R.T. 1999. *The Gospel According to Mathew. An Introduction and Commentary.* Leicester: IVP.

Fuellenbach, J. 2006. *The Kingdom of God: The Message of Jesus Today.* Eugene: Wipf & Stock.

Gellert, T. 2020. "Rise in Sexual Gender-Based Violence in Namibia Sparks Anti-Femicide Protests'. 28 October 2020. <theowp.org/rise-in-sexual-gender-based-violence-in-namibia-sparks-anti-femicide-protests/>; date of access: 12.12.2020.

Graig, V.G. 2000. *The Essence of the Church: A Community Created by the Church.* Grand Rapids: Baker Books.

Green, J.B. 2013. 'The Kingdom of God / Heaven', in *Dictionary of Jesus and the Gospels.* Downers Grove: IVP Academic.

Green, M. 1988. *Matthew for Today: A Running Commentary on the Gospel According to St Matthew.* London: Hodder & Stoughton.

Greidanus, S. 1999. *Preaching Christ from the Old Testament: A Contemporary Hermeneutical Model.* Grand Rapids: Eerdmans.

Guder, L. 1998. *Missional Church a Vision for the Sending of the Church.* Grand Rapids: Eerdmans.

Gundry, R.H. 1982. *Matthew: A Commentary on His Literary and Theological Art.* Grand Rapids: Eerdmans.

Gushee, D.P. & Stassen, G.H. 2016. *Kingdoms Ethics: Following Jesus in Contemporary Context.* Grand Rapids: Eerdmans.

Hagner, D.A. 1993. *World Biblical Commentary: Matthew 1-13.* Nashville: Thomas Nelson Publishers.

Hagner, D.A. 1997. 'Ethics and the Sermon on the Mount'. *Studia Theologica* 51:44-59.

Hagner, D.A. 2008. 'Holiness and Ecclesiology: The Church in Matthew', in *Upon the Rock: Studies in the Gospel of Matthew.* Gurtner, D.M. & Nolland, J. (eds). Grand Rapids: Eerdmans.

Hauerwas, S. 1993. 'Living a Proclaimed Reign of God: A Sermon on the Mount'. *Interpretation* 47(2):152-158.

Henley, J. 2019. 'Bribery Allegations of Fishing Rights Rock Iceland and Namibia'. *The Guardian* 15.11.2019. <theguardian.com/world/2019/nov/15/bribery-allegations-over-fishing-rights-rock-iceland-and-namibia>; date of access; 11.12.2020.

Henry, M. 2010. *The Matthew Henry Commentary.* Grand Rapids: Zondervan.

Herzog, W.R. 1994. *Parables of Subversive Speech: Jesus as Pedagogue of the Oppressed*. Louisville: Westminster John Knox Press.

Hill, D. 1981. *The Gospel of Matthew*. Grand Rapids: Eerdmans.

Holtom, J. 2013. 'Ghandi's Interpretation of the Sermon on the Mount', in *The Oxford Handbook of the Reception History of the Bible*. Lieb, M., Mason E. & Roberts, J. (eds). Oxford: Oxford University Press.

Houlden, L. 2003. *Jesus in History, Thought and Culture: An Encyclopedia, Vol. 1*. Santa Barbara: ABC-CLIO.

Hultgren, A.J. 2000. *The Parables of Jesus: A Commentary*. Grand Rapids: Eerdmans.

Kapolyo, J. 2006. 'Matthew', in *Africa Bible Commentary*. Adeyemo, T. (ed). Grand Rapids: Zondervan.

Keathley, K. 2010. *Salvation and Sovereignty: A Molinist Approach*. Nashville: B & H Publishing.

Keener, C.S. 1997. *Matthew*. Downers Grove: IVP.

Kennard, D.W. *Messiah Jesus: Christology in His Day and Ours*. New York: Peter Lang.

Kotva, J.J. 1996. *The Christian Case for Virtue Ethics*. Washington: Georgetown University Press.

Ladd, G.E. 1959. *The Gospel of the Kingdom: Scriptural Studies in the Kingdom of God*. Grand Rapids: Eerdmans.

Ladd, G.E. 1964. *Gospel of the Kingdom: Scriptural Studies in the Kingdom of God*. Grand Rapids: Eerdmans.

Ladd, G.E 1993. *A Theology of the New Testament*. Grand Rapids: Eerdmans.

Ladd, G.E. 2001. 'Kingdom of Christ, God, Heaven. *Terminology*', in *Evangelical Dictionary of Theology*. Elwell, W.A. (ed.). Grand Rapids: Baker Academic.

Ladd, G.E. 2002. *The Presence of the Future: The Eschatology of Biblical Realism*. Grand Rapids: Eerdmans.

Lawrence, A.B. 2017. *Comparative Characterization in the Sermon on the Mount: Characterization of the Ideal Disciple*. Eugene: Wipf & Stock.

Lawson, D. 2009. 'Transforming Initiatives: Leadership Ethics from the Sermon on the Mount'. *Journal of Applied Christian Leadership* 3(1):28-45.

Lawson, M. 2000. *Living by God's Master Plan: the Reality of the Kingdom of God from Eden to Revelation*. Fearn: Christian Focus.

Limpricht, C. 2012. 'Churches in Rehoboth', in *Rehoboth, Namibia - Past & Present*. Limpricht, C. (ed). Hamburg: Cornelia Limpricht.

Lingenfelter, S. 2008. *Leading Cross-culturally: Covenant Relationships for Effective Christian Leadership*. Grand Rapids: Baker Academic.

Lloyd-Jones, D.M. 2002. *Studies in the Sermon on the Mount*. Nottingham: IVP.

Lovin, R.W. 2011. *An Introduction to Christian Ethics*. Nashville: Abingdon Press.

Lundbom, J.R. 2009. 'At What Elevation is Jesus' Sermon on the Mount?' *Currents in Theology and Mission* 36(6):440-454.

Matthias, L.R. 2015. *The Cry of The Teacher's Soul*. Eugene: Wipf & Stock.

Mbewe, C. 2011. *Foundations of the Flock: Truths about the Church for All the Saints*. Hannibal: Granted Ministries Press.

McGrath, A.E. 1998. *Christian Theology: An Introduction*. Oxford: Blackwell.

McKnight, S. 2013. *Sermon on the Mount*. Grand Rapids: Zondervan.

McKnight, S. 2014. *Kingdom Conspiracy: Returning to the Radical Mission of the Local Church*. Grand Rapids: Brazos Press.

Moltmann, J. 1993. *The Way of Christ: Christology in Messianic Dimensions*. Minneapolis: Fortress Press.

Morgan, G.C. 1954. *The Gospel According to Matthew*. London: Oliphants.

Morton, R. 2010. 'Bultmann, Rudolf', in *Encyclopedia of the Historical Jesus*. Evans, C.A. (ed). London: Routledge.

Mounce, R.H. 1998. *Matthew: New International Biblical Commentary*. Peabody: Hendrickson.

National Planning Commission undated. 'The Root Causes of Poverty'. Windhoek: National Planning Commission. <www.npc.gov.na/download/pbriefs/rootcauses.pdf>; date of access: 12.12.2020.

New Era Staff Reporter, 2016. 'A Conversation with…The 'Pope of Rehoboth' Cares Deeply for the Youth'. *New Era*, 18th July 2016.

Newman, S. 2010. 'Books Review: Jonathan T. Pennington. *Heaven and Earth in the Gospel of Matthew*'. *Themelios* 35(2):298-300.

Nkansah-Obrempong, J. 2013. *Foundations for African Theological Ethics*. Carlisle: Langham Monographs.

Osborne, G.R. 2010. *Matthew*. Grand Rapids: Zondervan.

Pannenberg, W. 1969. *Theology and the Kingdom of God*. Louisville: Westminster John Knox Press.

Pennington, J.T. 2007. *Heaven and Earth in the Gospel of Matthew*. Leiden: Brill.

Phillipps, F.O. 2013.*Understanding the Church: God's Alternative Society: The Place for Spirit-Led Living*. Bloomington: WestBow Press.

Phiri, I.A. 2006. 'Rape', in *Africa Bible Commentary*. Adeyemo, T. (ed.). Grand Rapids: Zondervan.

Plummer R.L. 2010. *40 Questions about Interpreting the Bible*. Grand Rapids: Kregel.

Pohor, R. 2006. 'Tribalism, Ethnicity and Race'. *Africa Bible Commentary*. Adeyemo, T. (ed). Grand Rapids: Zondervan.

Przybylski, B. 2004. *Righteousness in Matthew and his World of Thought*. Cambridge: Cambridge University Press.

Quarles, C. 2011. *Sermon on the Mount: Restoring Christ's Message to the Modern Church*. Nashville: B&H Publishing.

Ridderbos, H.N. 1962. *The Coming of the Kingdom*. Philadelphia: The Presbyterian and Reformed Publishing Company.

Schaff, P. 2010. *History of the Christian Church, Vol. II.* -: Revelation Insight Publishing.

Segal, R.A. 2006. 'Myth', in *Companion to the Study of Religion*. Segal, R.A. (ed). Oxford: Blackwell.

Shaw, M. 1996. *The Kingdom of God in Africa*. Grand Rapids: Baker Book House Company.

Siker, J.S. 1997. *Scripture and Ethics: Twentieth-Century Portrays*. New York: Oxford University Press.

Simmons, B.E. 1992. 'Preaching Ideas from the Sermon on the Mount'. *The Theological Educator* 46:125-132.

Smith, J.-M. 2011. 'Rehoboth police crack down on drinking and crime'. *The Namibian* 06.05.2011.
https://www.namibian.com.na/index.php?id=79437&page=archive-read;
Date of access: 05.12.2020.

Snyder, H.A. 2001. *Models of the Kingdom*. Eugene: Wipf & Stock.

Soungalo, S. 2006. 'James', in Africa Bible Commentary. Adeyemo, T. (ed.). Grand Rapids: Zondervan.

Stanton, G. 2001. 'Message and Miracles', in *Cambridge Companion to Jesus*. Bockmuehl, M. (ed). Cambridge: Cambridge University Press.

Steele, D.N. & Thomas, C.C. 1963. *The Five Points of Calvinism: Defined, Defended, Documented*. Phillipsburg: Presbyterian & Reformed Publishing.

Stein, R.H. 1994. *The Method and Message of Jesus' Teachings*. Louisville: Westminster John Knox Press.

Stott, J. 2000. *The Message of the Sermon on the Mount*. Leicester: IVP.

Talbert, C.H. 2004. 'Is it with Ethics that the Sermon on the Mount is Concerned?', in *Literary Encounters with the Reign of God*. Ringe, S.H. & Kim, H.C.P. (eds). London: T & T Clark International.

The Urban Trust of Namibia, 2013. *Building Safe and Caring Communities: Safety Audit Report Rehoboth*. Windhoek: The Urban Trust of Namibia.

The World Bank. *Does Fiscal Policy benefit the Poor and Reduce Inequality in Namibia?* Washington: International Bank for Reconstruction and Development / The World Bank.

Tolonen, M. 2013. *Witness is Presence: Reading Stanley Hauerwas in a Nordic Setting*. Eugene: Wipf & Stock.

Troftgruben, T.M. 2020. 'Prayer and Ethics in the Sermon on the Mount'. *Word & World* 40(3):227-235.

Varkey, M. 2017. *Salvation in Continuity: Reconsidering Matthew's Soteriology*. Minneapolis: Fortress Press.

Wiersbe, W.W. 2007. *The Wiersbe Bible Commentary: New Testament*. Colorado Springs: David C. Cook.

Wilkins, M.J. 2004. *The NIV Application Commentary: Matthew*. Grand Rapids: Zondervan.

Willson, T.R. 2014. *Reclaiming the Kingdom of God Metaphor for the Twenty-first Century Church*. Portland: George Fox University.

Woodall, C. 2012. *Kingdom: The Expression of God's Rule*. Eugene: Wipf & Stock.

Wright, T. 2002. *Matthew for Everyone, Part 1, Chapters 1-15*. London: SPCK.

Zandberg. J. 2009. 'An Investigation into a Large Number of Churches in Rehoboth'. <rehobothbasters.org/images/stories/Books_Reports/thelargenumbersofchurchesin rehoboth.pdf>; date of access: 11.12.2020.

- 2004. *CMA Rehoboth Block B Report*. Rehoboth: Health Communication Partnership.

- 2016. 'The Kingdom of God', in *Africa Study Bible*, Jusu, J. (ed.). Wheaton: Oasis International.

- 'Kingdom', in *Cambridge Dictionary*. Cambridge: Cambridge University Press. <dictionary.cambridge.org/de/worterbuch.englisch/kingdom>; date of access: 11.12.2020.

- *Cambridge Dictionary*, 'Kingdom', http://dictionary.cambridge.org/de/worterbuch/englisch/kingdom; date of access: 15.09.2017.

# Questionnaire

**1.** Please name the three most significant social challenges which can be observed in the Rehoboth community:


**2.** Do you agree or disagree with the following statement?

"The lifestyles of many church members in Rehoboth do not reflect the ethical standards which are set by the teachings of the Bible."

Please tick

    I agree      ☐

    I disagree   ☐


**3.** Do you agree or disagree with the following statement regarding the way Christians should live:

"Jesus emphasized that his true followers, the citizens of God's kingdom, were to be entirely different from others."

Please tick

    I agree      ☐

    I disagree   ☐


**4.** What percentage of Christians in Rehoboth live out kingdom ethics?

Answer: ......%

**5.** In his Sermon on the Mount (Matthew 5:1 -7:29) Jesus deals with a number of ethical issues.

● Which of these issues are the most relevant ones for the community in Rehoboth at large?


● Which of these issues are the most relevant ones for the members of your church?


**6.** If you had to address one particular ethical issue in your next sermon which one would you choose. Please choose <u>only one</u>:

Murder          □

Adultery        □

Divorce         □

Poverty         □

Greed            □

Judgemental Spirit   □

Materialism       □


**7.** How often have you preached on a passage from Jesus' Sermon on the Mount (Matthew 5:1 -7:29)?

● within the last year             ….. times

● within the last two years       ….. times

● within the last three years     ….. times

**8.** With which of the following statements do you agree? Please tick (only once)

•The heart of Jesus' teachings centres around the theme of the Church whose head is Jesus Christ.   □

•The heart of Jesus's teaching centres around the theme of the Kingdom of God.  □

**9.** Do you agree or disagree with the following statement:

"Preaching on ethical issues can transform the lives of Christians in Rehoboth!"

Please tick!

I agree       □

I disagree    □

What passages would you choose? Please name three passages:

**10.** How would you define the *Kingdom of God*?

**11.** With which of the following statements do you agree? Please tick!

The expressions *Kingdom of God* and *kingdom of Heaven* refer to two different realities □

The expressions *Kingdom of God* and *kingdom of Heaven* refer to the same reality. □

**12.**  With which of the following statements do you agree? Please tick!

•The basic meaning of the expression *Kingdom of God* is *territory of God*  □

•The basic meaning of the expression *Kingdom of God* is *church of God*   □

•The basic meaning of the expression *Kingdom of God* is *rule of God*.    □

**13.** Do you agree or disagree with the following statement?

"We are living in an age when the Kingdom of God is already here but not yet fully here."

Please tick!

I agree      □

I disagree      □


**14.** Which of the following statements do you think are correct? Please tick!

●It is the task of the church to establish the Kingdom of God. □

●It is God's work to establish the Kingdom of God.        □


**15.** Which are the most important ethical principles which we can find in Jesus' Sermon on the Mount?

# Namibian Theological Research Papers

## Volume 1

*Themes in African Church History: Missionary Motives, Merits and Mistakes* (2019)
Anthony Brendell & Thorsten Prill


## Volume 2

*The Namibian Church and Money: A Biblical Perspective* (2020)
Johann van Wyk & Thorsten Prill


## Volume 3

*The Kingdom of God and the Christian Community in Rehoboth: The Sermon on the Mount and its Relevance for the Namibian Church* (2021)
Heinz Mouton


Serious Editor: Dr Thorsten Prill

Contact:
Edinburgh Bible College (EBC)
39 Greendykes Road
Broxburn EH52 5AF
Scotland
thorsten@edinburghbiblecollege.co.uk